The Miracles of Jesus

Finding the Extraordinary in the Everyday, Ordinary

Jared K. Pearson, MD

Copyright © 2024 Jared Kevin Pearson All rights reserved

This work is not an official publication of The Church of Jesus Christ of Latter-Day Saints. The views expressed herein are the responsibility of the author and do not represent the position of the Church.

Images used in this book were obtained from commons.wikimedia.org under common use laws and are not under copyright.

No part of this book may be reproduced, or stored in a retrieval system, or transmitted in any form or by any means, electronic, mechanical, photocopying, recording, or otherwise, without express written permission of the publisher.

Any comments, questions, concerns, or clarifications can be directed to jared.pearson@gmail.com. Please put "Miracles of Jesus" in the subject line.

ISBN-13: 979-8-9899585-1-1 (paperback)

Library of Congress Control Number: 2024901805

Cover design by: Jared Pearson

Cover photo: view of Mount Timpanogos on a winter trail run from the mountains south of Heber Valley.

Printed in the United States of America

Contents

Introduction 4
Letter to the Reader 9
Jesus Turns Water into Wine 12
Jesus Heals Fevers 21
The Miracle of the Fishes.. 30
Jesus Casts out Evil Spirits..................................... 43
Jesus Heals a Leper... 59
Jesus Heals the Paralytic.. 72
Jesus Raises the Dead... 85
Jesus Stills the Storm... 99
Jesus Heals the Woman with an Issue of Blood........ 111
Jesus Heals the Blind... 125
Jesus Heals a Withered Hand................................. 143
Jesus Heals the Hearing and Speech Impaired Man.. 152
Jesus Heals the Man with Dropsy............................ 163
Jesus Feeds the Multitude......................................172
Afterword.. 183
About The Author.. 184

Introduction

This project has long been a labor of love. Its genesis began in 2019 after hearing a BYU speech by Elder Lawrence Corbridge, then a General Authority Seventy of the Church of Jesus Christ of Latter-day Saints. His talk titled "Stand Forever" focused on grounding your belief firmly in the pertinent primary questions of the gospel and not becoming distracted by the endless array of secondary questions. Near the end of his speech, with passion and conviction, he urged everyone to simply believe. To believe that with God all things are possible. And the occasional extraordinary, often dubbed miraculous, should not become a stumbling block to our faith. In reality, the everyday ordinary is far more impressive. He states:

> "While it is understandable that we may be challenged by the extraordinary, we shouldn't be, because ordinary things are actually far more phenomenal.
> The most phenomenal occurrences of all time and eternity—the most amazing wonders, the most astounding, awesome developments—are the most common and widely recognized. They include: I am; you are; we are; and all that we perceive exists as well, from subatomic particles to the farthest reaches of the cosmos and everything in between, including all of the wonders of life. Is there anything greater than those ordinary realities? No. Nothing else even comes close. You can't begin to imagine, much less describe, anything greater than what already is.
> In light of what is, nothing else should surprise us. It should be easy to believe that with God all things are possible.
> The healing of the withered hand is not nearly as amazing as the existence of the hand in the first place.

If it exists, it follows that it can certainly be fixed when it is broken. The greater event is not in its healing but in its creation.

More phenomenal than resurrection is birth. The greater wonder is not that life, having once existed, could come again but that it ever exists at all.

More amazing than raising the dead is that we live at all. A silent heart that beats again is not nearly as amazing as the heart that beats within your breast right now.

How can you believe in extraordinary things... Easy, just look around and believe."

His words penetrated the depths of my soul. In an effort to acknowledge the complexities of God, accept His will and timing, and more fully comprehend His love not just for all human beings but especially for ME, I realized I too had looked beyond the mark. In looking for a yet unseen miracle I was missing the miracle of what I could see.

At the time of his speech, I was four months out from ankle surgery complicated by a permanent nerve injury. Although I would say that I had been walking through my valley of the shadow of death, that would be inaccurate. Instead, I was scootering, crutching, and now limping - permanently trapped in my own valley of the shadow of death. A new normal. The damage to my lower leg nerve left me with months of debilitating pain, numbness, and weakness. Though the pain finally subsided, muscle weakness and numbness became my new reality. It was impossible to run and be active again. I began to feel depressed. I reflected time and time again on a priesthood blessing promising complete healing. But when the healing wasn't coming, I began to question my faith and, even at times, the existence of whom I was trying to have faith in. A dear friend reminded me early on that "God created your nerve, and He knows how to fix it." But, I would often want to scream in anger "Why wasn't he fixing it?!"

Elder Corbridge's words sunk deep into my heart in this state of frustration, doubt, and discouragement.

"[Your] healing…is not nearly as amazing as the existence of [your leg] in the first place…The greater event is not in its healing but in its creation."

I realized at that moment that I was missing out. Instead of appreciating and seeing the miracle of every day, I wallowed in self-pity as I waited and hoped for the miracle of healing. My desire to live for some unknown future event robbed me of my joy for what I had now. I began to feel that given my background as a physician and my desire to be a disciple of the master physician, I may have a unique perspective to offer others. A hope for those who might be seeking the extraordinary but are missing an appreciation of the ordinary.

As President Nelson began to speak of miracles[1] and promised miracles[2] my desire to work on this project grew and continued to take shape. Furthermore, as he urged members of the Church to learn about miracles[3] and then to seek and expect miracles[4] my desire to complete this project accelerated as we commenced studying His miracles in the New Testament as a Church in 2023.

"The Miracles of Jesus" takes you on a journey into the science of the seemingly ordinary - vision, hearing, speaking, walking, immune system, skin, nervous system, etc. After introducing the miracle in the scriptures, you will learn the "ordinary" about the ailment the Savior was able to heal and hopefully develop an appreciation for the ordinary existence in the first place. Then, in the spirit of Nephi who likened all scripture unto us that it might be for our profit and learning, both ordinary and miraculous aspects of each miracle will be applied for your spiritual profit and learning. Finally, you will be invited to reflect on and encouraged to apply what you have learned and draw nearer to the giver of all miracles, Jesus Christ.

What the Savior did for the people he met was miraculous. He raised the dead, cleansed the leper, cast out countless evil spirits, calmed the storm, caused the blind to see, the deaf to hear, the dumb to speak, the lame to walk, and much more. Even after His greatest miracle, that of His resurrection, His disciples continued to perform countless miracles in His name.

For many, a belief in these events known as miracles can seem, well, unbelievable. And if what Jesus did is difficult for some to believe, then it could be difficult for some to believe what he taught. And if it is difficult to believe what he taught, then it would be difficult to follow what he taught. And if it is difficult to follow what he taught, then it would be difficult to feel the joy that he promised because "happiness in life is most likely achieved when founded upon the teachings of the Lord Jesus Christ."[5] Since a significant purpose of our existence is to have joy,[6] it is critical to replace the potential stumbling block of the miraculous with something that builds faith in Jesus Christ and leads to that promised joy.

I hope this book offers an antidote to the unbeliever in all of us. As we begin to appreciate, understand, and revere the "ordinary" more fully, we will begin to see the extraordinary beauty, awe, and wonder of the ordinary. And if we see the ordinary as extraordinary, we may begin to realize that things just didn't come together by chance, and therefore, there must be a creator. And if we begin to believe in a creator then we might start to believe there is a purpose to His creations. And if this truth that there is a purpose to life begins to take root in our hearts, then we may soon recognize this creator has a plan for us.

As you seek out this plan you will eventually discover that Jesus Christ is central to the plan and critical to YOUR happiness. You will then begin to exercise faith in Jesus Christ by learning of Him and believing in Him. And then, with this faith in Jesus Christ, you will believe His miracles and see His miracles as evidence of His love for you. And because Jesus' love is infinite, and He and God are the same yesterday, today, and forever, exercising faith in Jesus Christ will allow miracles to occur in your own life NOW.

---

[1] Russell M. Nelson. "We Can Do Better and Be Better." General Conference, April 2019

[2] Russell M. Nelson. "Hear Him." General Conference, April 2020

[3] Russell M. Nelson. "Christ Is Risen; Faith in Him will Move Mountains." General Conference, April 2021

[4] Russell M. Nelson. "The Power of Spiritual Momentum." General Conference, April 2022

[5] Family: A Proclamation to the World

[6] 2 Nephi 2:25

Letter to the Reader

Jesus Christ ministers to the one. He meets each individual where they are and enables them to become better. His desire and power to bless the children of God were a miracle for the countless lives He touched while He walked the earth. As the Living Christ, modern apostles testify,

> "He walked the roads of Palestine, healing the sick, causing the blind to see, and raising the dead."[1]

Jesus Christ is the same healer today as He was when He walked the earth. His "hand is outstretched still."[2] He desires to bless you and me. He will perform miracles in OUR life. Miracles will occur according to our faith. The Savior taught,

> "For behold, I am God; and I am a God of miracles; and I will show unto the world that I am the same yesterday, today, and forever; and I work not among the children of men save it be according to their faith."[3]

Like Moroni of old, I write to "show unto you a God of miracles."[4] As you learn of the miracles of Jesus I invite you to ponder how your Savior continues to be a God of miracles in your life.   Mormon asks "Has the day of miracles ceased?"[5] No! It hasn't!   Elder Donald Hallstrom, former General Authority Seventy, encouraged,

> "Our supreme focus should be on the spiritual miracles that are available to all of God's children. No matter our ethnicity, no matter our nationality, no matter what we have done if we repent, no matter what may have been done to us—all of us have equal access to these miracles. We are living a miracle, and further miracles lie ahead."[6]

I affirm that God IS a God of miracles. He desires to work miracles in your life just as He has done in times of old. We each face personal challenges in life. They are necessary for our growth and development. At times these challenges may seem like immovable mountains. President Nelson taught that these

> "mountains may be loneliness, doubt, illness, or other personal problems..moving your mountains may require a miracle. Learn about miracles. Miracles come according to your faith in the Lord."[7]

As I have studied the miracles of Jesus and pondered their application in my life I have started to see the ordinary around me as extraordinary! As I have considered the miracles of Jesus and how they can apply to my own life, I have felt closer to the Savior. My faith in Him to move the mountains in my life has deepened. More particularly, I have felt his deep love and care for me. I have felt my heart soften as I have been blessed to feel the Savior's love for those around me.

As you learn of Him through the miracles that He performed, you, too, will more fully feel His deep love for you.

With Warmest Regards,
Jared Pearson

---

[1] The Living Christ

[2] 2 Nephi 19:21

[3] 2 Nephi 27:23

[4] Mormon 9:11

[5] Moroni 7:35

[6] "Has the Day of Miracles Ceased?" General Conference, October 2017

[7] "Christ Has Risen; Faith in Him Will Move Mountains." General Conference, April 2021

Chapter 1

Jesus Turns Water into Wine

Although, as a child, He had taught in the temple and likely many other times among his family and close associates, this time was different. He had now grown "grace for grace"[1] and was consequently endowed with power. He had fasted for 40 days and had conquered the temptations of Satan. He came to His cousin John insisting that He, a perfect being, be baptized in order to "fulfill all righteousness."[2] He was ready to proclaim the gospel, teach the way to obtain the kingdom of heaven, and perform many miracles along the way. This was the beginning of the three years of the Savior's mortal ministry.

The first documented miracle of Jesus is recorded only in the Gospel of John. At the beginning of the second chapter, Christ and His disciples were invited to a wedding. After the guests exhausted the supply of wine, His mother came to Jesus asking for help. Although he told his mother that his time had not yet come, Jesus loved his mother and told her he would do what she needed. His mother instructed the servants to do whatever Jesus told them to do. They filled pots with water and then drew from them as Jesus requested. However, instead of drawing water, they drew wine. The wine was so flavorful that the governor of the feast marveled at how they had saved the best-tasting wine for last.

The following is the King James version with the Joseph Smith Translation added for clarity in parenthesis:

> 1 And the third day there was a marriage in Cana of Galilee; and the mother of Jesus was there:
> 2 And both Jesus was called, and his disciples, to the marriage.
> 3 And when they wanted wine, the mother of Jesus saith unto him, They have no wine.

4 Jesus saith unto her, (Woman, what wilt thou have me to do for thee? that will I do; for mine hour is not yet come)

5 His mother saith unto the servants, Whatsoever he saith unto you, do it.

6 And there were set there six waterpots of stone, after the manner of the purifying of the Jews, containing two or three firkins apiece.

7 Jesus saith unto them, Fill the waterpots with water. And they filled them up to the brim.

8 And he saith unto them, Draw out now, and bear unto the governor of the feast. And they bare it.

9 When the ruler of the feast had tasted the water that was made wine, and knew not whence it was: (but the servants which drew the water knew;) the governor of the feast called the bridegroom,

10 And saith unto him, Every man at the beginning doth set forth good wine; and when men have well drunk, then that which is worse: but thou hast kept the good wine until now.

11 This beginning of miracles did Jesus in Cana of Galilee, and manifested forth his glory; and his disciples believed on Him.

Faith of Jesus' Mother, Mary, and Her Servants

This first miracle gives us a unique insight into the faith of Jesus' mother, Mary. She understood that she gave birth to the Son of God who created both the heavens[3] and the earth.[4] She knew that "all things were made by Him."[5] She must have understood the scriptures well; if her son could form mountains[6] and could simply speak and make the world[7] then surely He could, by some power, command the elements to make wine.[8] She knew that Jesus was the Son of God and, therefore, trusted in the words that would be proclaimed from her son's mouth. She encouraged the banquet servants to have this same trust. She exhorted them to do whatever He asked them to do.

The pots were filled with 2-3 firkins of water. A firkin is equivalent to about 9 gallons of water, and therefore, each pot holds about 18 to 27 gallons of water. Given there were 6 pots, there was a total of 100 to 160 gallons of water. However, these were not ordinary water pots. John states that the large pots of water were there "after the manner of the purifying of the Jews."[9] In other words, it was also customary in the Jewish tradition to wash one's hands prior to eating. John seems to suggest that the original purpose of these pots was to hold water that was to be used to clean the hands and feet of the guests. Jesus was now asking to fill those same water pots for the guests to drink wine.

Turning water into wine is a miracle, but transforming water in pots that were likely previously intended to clean dirt off the guests into wine that the governor would call "good wine" is even more miraculous. Equally miraculous is the faith of the servants to not only draw up water turned into wine to serve to the guests but to draw from pots that likely held water with a cleansing purpose now converted to a drinking purpose.

The Miracle of Water and the Everyday

Water is a relatively simple structure. Two hydrogen atoms are bound together with one oxygen atom to form a water molecule. Atoms consist of neutral elements called neutrons, positively charged elements called protons, and negatively charged elements called electrons. The goal of each atom is to have a specific number of electrons that orbit around the nucleus of protons in order to be complete. Each hydrogen atom has one extra electron and oxygen is short two electrons. Bringing together two hydrogens with one oxygen to make H_2O is a perfect match. However, water is unique in that the negatively charged electrons tend to spend more time around the oxygen atom than the hydrogen atoms. This creates a slightly negative charge on the side of the oxygen and a slightly positive charge on the hydrogen atom known as water polarity.

Water polarity allows for other molecules, such as oxygen, to dissolve into the water. Without oxygen dissolving in water, life in the ocean would cease to exist. Water polarity also attracts water molecules to one another. The slightly positively charged hydrogen side is attracted to the slightly negative oxygen side, helping water molecules stick to one another by a force called cohesion and stick to other things by the force of adhesion. This allows water to move through the roots and stems of plants and the blood vessels of animals. As one molecule moves, it pulls another along with it.

Water is one of the only natural elements that can exist in all three states of matter on the earth at the same time - solid, liquid, and gas. When water freezes, the hydrogen bonds hold water molecules further apart making it less dense than liquid. This means water is the only molecule on earth that floats when transforming from a liquid to a solid. If water didn't float, lakes and rivers would freeze solid, and animal and plant life in lakes would die every winter. Because of its relatively low boiling point, ocean and lake water can evaporate into water vapor, form clouds, and travel long distances to provide rain to life around the earth. Furthermore, evaporated water can fall as mountain snow during the winter time and slowly melt in spring to provide a steady source of summer water to the valley below.

Jesus Christ created water to bless our lives on earth. It literally sustains life. The very fact that water exists and behaves the way it does despite its very simple chemical structure is truly a miracle. In this first miracle, it can be easy to focus solely on the miracle of the finished product - the wine. However, one must also look at the miracle that the ingredients for wine even exist, namely water, grapes, and stone pots. President Howard W. Hunter taught,

"But poor, indeed, was the making of the wine in the pots of stone, compared with its original making in the beauty of the vine and the abundance of the swelling grapes. No one could explain the onetime miracle at the wedding feast, but then neither could they explain the everyday miracle of the splendor of the vineyard itself."[10]

President Hunter cautions us that when looking for miracles in our life if we focus solely on the final product - the miracle - we may fail to appreciate the miracle of the everyday. In other words, if in our journey to climb mountains our focus is solely on the summit, we risk missing the beauty and miracle of the journey. When seeking miracles in our own life we must not overlook "ordinary" miracles along the path. A story from my own life illustrates this principle.

In 2018 I went canyoneering with my wife and four other friends in Zions National Park. The day began with a 280-foot rappel into Englestead Slot Canyon followed by many other rappels in and out of water as we descended into the top of the Zion Narrows. It was my first time canyoneering and the beauty mixed with terror was spectacular. However, just as we were entering the top of the narrows, I jumped off a small ledge into a shallow muddy pool. Immediately I felt a pop and a crunch and buckled to the ground. I had broken one of the bones in my lower leg and tore the ligament that connected it to the other lower leg bone. I was unable to put weight on my leg without excruciating pain. It was late in the afternoon and we were cold, hungry, and many miles from the parking lot. Attempts to hop on one leg through the moving water were impossible. We prayed for help and needed a miracle.

Shortly after it happened, we saw two people walking ahead of us with walking sticks. I had the impression to ask to borrow them. A friend expertly used climbing supplies to weave a stretcher between the two walking poles that I could lay on to be carried out. Kind travelers joined our group to help carry me. Others ran ahead and contacted the park rangers through the park shuttle radio who came in the time of need with food and other supplies. Seven hours after the injury, we were finally out of the canyon.

After my injury, I received a blessing of healing. However, after surgery, I experienced a complication that led to nerve damage, leaving me with foot drop, excruciating nerve pain that was relentless for months, and persistent uncomfortable numbness in my foot. I was disappointed and, at times, angry that a miracle had not occurred on my behalf. Looking back, however, I realize I was focusing on the wine. In other words, I was looking past the miracle of the rescue and only focusing on the result of being healed.

Since the accident, I can now more fully appreciate the everyday miracles that occurred on that day. The miracle of friends who walked with me and helped carry me in my time of need. These strangers were like the good Samaritan who came to offer help and support. Adversity, physical pain, and suffering have taken on value. It has given me more empathy and compassion for people who are experiencing pain in all its forms and has allowed me to bring some measure of comfort to those people in their time of need. I no longer need the miracle that I was seeking to occur in my own life. I have been able to better appreciate the everyday miracles along the journey.

You: Turning water into wine

The water in those pots first became dirty to clean the banquet guests, but then later, that same element of water was turned into wine. What areas of your life are dirtied that could be cleansed by water from the water pots? How have the cares of the world taken you from your pure form when you were born and figuratively dirtied you on your journey of life? How can you more fully surrender your will and turn over the impure elements of your nature to the Savior? We can partake of the water each week as we make covenants during the ordinance of the sacrament. As we promise to be willing to take upon us His name, to always remember Him, and to keep His commandments, we are promised that we may always have His Spirit to be with us. The Spirit has a purifying and cleansing power. Not only does the Savior's living water have a cleansing power, but if the Savior can perform the miracle of turning water into the best-tasting wine, what enabling power and miracles can the Savior perform for you in YOUR life? How can He take the unclean areas of your life and turn them figuratively into best-tasting wine? How can you allow the Savior to take your mortal being, purify it, and make it be more fully changed for "good?" Jesus Christ's atonement has the power to transform and change us just like he transformed the water into wine. King Benjamin taught this powerful principle.

> "For the natural man is an enemy to God, and has been from the fall of Adam, and will be, forever and ever, unless he yields to the enticings of the Holy Spirit, and putteth off the natural man and becometh a saint through the atonement of Christ the Lord, and becometh as a child, submissive, meek, humble, patient, full of love, willing to submit to all things which the Lord seeth fit to inflict upon him, even as a child doth submit to his father."[11]

Wine is a complex liquid solution. Although water and ethyl alcohol comprise 98% of wine, 800-1000 different chemicals make up the remaining 2 percent. The variations in this small percentage contribute to the wide variety of colors and flavors. The Savior perfectly understood what exact combination of all of these chemicals would produce the best outcome. Similarly, the Savior is ready and willing to help you with the complex issues of your life. He profoundly understands you, and knows what combinations of life's experiences, trials, and challenges can be mixed to produce the best outcome for us! When we turn ourselves over to Him and trust Him, He is both willing and able to help. Choosing to let God prevail in your life means you are "willing to let God be the most important influence in [our] life," and allow "His words, His commandments, and His covenants [to] influence what you do each day."[12]

Considering the critical mission of the Savior, it may come as a surprise to some that something so trivial as providing wine for guests at a wedding banquet was the first miracle the Savior of the world performed on this earth. However, this first miracle demonstrates that the Savior not only cares about our spiritual pressures in life but also the temporal. He perfectly understands the pressures we face in the routines of life as we seek to balance personal, family, and professional responsibilities. He offered in a real and tangible way to help his mother's burdens become light. He deeply cares about the routine pressures, burdens, and responsibilities we have in our temporal life and if we reach out to Him and trust Him, he will perform miracles to help us.

Reflection
1. Make a list of the roles and responsibilities that you have. Make a list of Christ-like attributes.
2. Consider what Christ-like attributes could better assist you as you fulfill your current roles and responsibilities.
3. Choose one Christ-like attribute to study and develop this month. Reflect on the changes you see as you seek to become more Christ-like.

---

[1] John 1:16, D&C 93:12-13

[2] Matthew 3:15

[3] Psalms 33:6

[4] Jeremiah 51:15

[5] John 1:3

[6] Amos 4:13

[7] Doctrine and Covenants 38:3

[8] Doctrine and Covenants 117:6

[9] John 2:6

[10] Howard W. Hunter. "The God that Doest Wonders." General Conference, April 1989

[11] Mosiah 3:19

[12] Russell M. Nelson. "Let God Prevail." General Conference, October 2020

Chapter 2

Jesus Heals Fevers
Jesus Heals a Nobleman's Son of Capernaum

Following the miracle of turning water into wine, the Savior traveled from Galilee to Jerusalem for the Passover. After two days, he returned to Galilee by traveling through Samaria. He met the woman at the well, testified of his divinity, and taught her and the people there. When he returned to Galilee, he was received by many of the same people who had attended the feast and witnessed the miracle of water turning into wine.

Upon returning, he met a nobleman seeking the Savior to heal his son, who was on the brink of death. He implored the Savior to come to Capernaum. Without seeing or touching his son, the Savior told him to "go thy way; thy son liveth."[1] When the noble father returned, his servants met him, rejoicing, saying his son was healed and that his fever had left him. He discovered that his son was healed at the same hour - the seventh hour, to be exact - that the Savior had pronounced that his son lived. In John chapter 4, we read:

> 46 So Jesus came again into Cana of Galilee, where he made the water wine. And there was a certain nobleman, whose son was sick at Capernaum.
> 47 When he heard that Jesus was come out of Judæa into Galilee, he went unto him, and besought him that he would come down, and heal his son: for he was at the point of death.
> 48 Then said Jesus unto him, Except ye see signs and wonders, ye will not believe.
> 49 The nobleman saith unto him, Sir, come down ere my child die.

50 Jesus saith unto him, Go thy way; thy son liveth. And the man believed the word that Jesus had spoken unto him, and he went his way.

51 And as he was now going down, his servants met him, and told him, saying, Thy son liveth.

52 Then inquired he of them the hour when he began to amend. And they said unto him, Yesterday at the seventh hour the fever left him.

53 So the father knew that it was at the same hour, in the which Jesus said unto him, Thy son liveth: and himself believed, and his whole house.

54 This is again the second miracle that Jesus did, when he was come out of Judæa into Galilee.

John's account of this miracle seems to emphasize the timing regarding the pronouncement of healing and the actual healing despite the large distance between the two events. Therefore, an explanation of time and distances might be helpful. At the time of Jesus, the Jews regarded a new day as six hours different than what we do today. We consider midnight, or 0:00, as the beginning of a new day and noon as the day's midpoint. Each hourly time point is placed from these two reference times. In other words, the seventh hour in modern times would mean either 7 am or 7 pm. However, the Jews refer to a new day beginning at what we currently would refer to as 6 pm. This stems from the first book of Genesis, which states that "the evening and the morning were the first day."[2] Hence, Shabbat (the Jewish sabbath occurring on Saturday) begins at sundown (about 6 pm) on Friday and extends 24 hrs until sundown on Saturday. Hourly time references from the 6 am and 6 pm starting points would mean that the seventh hour would either be 1 am or 1 pm in modern-day timing. Therefore, according to Jewish time, the seventh hour would be 6 am or pm plus 7 hours, and therefore most likely at 1 pm our time.

However, the distance between Cana and Capernaum is about 17 miles, and the terrain is challenging to travel in one day of daylight. If this miracle occurred according to Jewish times, it would have been impossible to leave Capernaum safely early enough to receive the Savior's pronouncement of healing at 1:00 pm. Similarly, it would be unwise to venture the 17 miles back home after receiving the Savior's pronouncement. Therefore, one must consider that the Gospel of John was the last written gospel in the Bible and is believed to have been written around 85 AD. By this time, Roman influences on time were appearing frequently. Furthermore, given that one of John's objectives in writing his gospel was to testify that Jesus is the Christ to the Gentiles, he likely referenced time in a way that they would understand by following midnight and noon.

In this context, the seventh hour would most likely mean 7 pm which many biblical scholars believe to be more accurate. It is more likely that the nobleman traveled all day and met Jesus at 7 pm, stayed with friends that evening, and then traveled back the next day and met his servants midday, who were coming to bring the joyous news from the prior evening that the fever left him "yesterday at the seventh hour" according to the Roman timing. By including this precise detail of the pronounced time for healing and the observed time of healing 17 miles apart, John seems to emphasize the immediate healing ability of the Savior.

Jesus Heals Peter's mother-in-law of a fever

In Matthew 8:14-15, Mark 1:30-31, and Luke 4:38-39 we learn how Jesus also healed Peter's mother-in-law who was sick with fever. In Mark's account, the disciple brothers Simon Peter and Andrew, along with James and John, had just witnessed the Savior teach in the synagogue and cast out devils before arriving at Peter's house. Here is the simple account in Mark 1:30-31.

> 30 But Simon's wife's mother lay sick of a fever, and anon they tell him of her.
> 31 And he came and took her by the hand, and lifted her up; and immediately the fever left her, and she ministered unto them.

Unlike the nobleman's son, who was healed from afar, Jesus went into the bedroom of Simon's mother-in-law to heal her. Rather than pronouncing the words of healing as he did to the nobleman who came unto Jesus, Jesus came unto Simon's mother-in-law, took her by the hand, and healed her. After she was ministered to by the Savior, she could, in turn, minister back to them.

To perform such a miracle, whether from a great distance like the nobleman's son or in person like Peter's mother-in-law, the Savior had to have not only a complete understanding of the complexities of fever but also know how to resolve it.

The Complexity of Fever

Fever is a simple measurement of a complex internal response initiated by our body's immune system. Fever is a sign in many disease processes and often occurs in response to a viral or bacterial infection. Our bodies normally have a temperature set point of about 37 degrees Celsius. The body uses proteins called cytokines to raise its temperature and optimize its immune response, which is typically at temperatures higher than 38 degrees.

Over sixty cytokines, known as interleukins, play an integral role in activating, regulating, and terminating the body's immune response. Cytokines are the body's communication mechanism to coordinate with the rest of the immune system. These cytokines help prepare the body to mount an immune response to a possible threat. When these cells encounter foreign substances in the body, such as viruses or bacteria, they release many cytokines, including interleukin-1. Interleukin-1 (IL-1) is produced by immune cells called monocytes, macrophages, and T cells. The role of IL-1 is to increase the normal temperature set point of the body from 37 degrees Celsius to a higher temperature. The temperature is maintained by altering the balance of heat production and heat loss regulated in a small part of the brain called the hypothalamus. The hypothalamus maintains this higher temperature until the immune response is successful.

Overproduction or underproduction of cytokines can lead to severe illness. Overproduction has been implicated in causing severe systemic diseases such as sepsis, shock, and multi-system organ failure. This so-called "cytokine storm" can quickly make a healthy person sick. Conversely, an insufficient response to an infection can cause an infection to take hold and lead to life-threatening illness. This can occur when people are on medications that suppress the immune system or when diseases attack the immune system and prevent it from working properly. An example of this is HIV which causes Acquired Immune Deficiency Syndrome (AIDS). Immune system dysfunction allows viruses or bacteria that are usually kept in check to take hold of the body's system and lead to severe illness.

The body's immune system is so complex that an entire branch of medicine known as immunology is dedicated to the seemingly innumerable proteins, signals, cells, receptors, and processes involved in keeping our bodies healthy. Our body's immune response, which usually functions appropriately without a single thought day after day, is truly a miracle. The fact that we have been able to begin to understand some of these processes and study them is also truly a miracle. This has led to targeted therapies that help treat cancer while preserving quality of life by minimizing medication side effects. A deeper understanding of our immune system has also led to the development of medications and vaccines to cure and prevent infection, along with clones of antibodies that slow or terminate the debilitating effects of auto-immune disease.

Healing, in the Lord's time

The fact that the timing of Jesus speaking to the nobleman "Go thy way; thy son liveth" and the fever leaving his son were at the "same hour" emphasizes Jesus as the master physician. The Creator of the earth, the One who knows when a sparrow falls from a tree, surely has intelligence for interleukins. Surely, he comprehends the cytokine storm. Without a doubt, he is a master of monocytes and macrophages, triumphs over T-cell mediated responses, has the smarts for cell signaling, has power innately in immunoregulation, and is the master regulator over receptor-mediated responses.

More than a perfect understanding of all these processes that are written about in dozens of textbooks, each hundreds of pages long, is this: at the very given moment in time, the Savior knew where this nobleman's child and where Peter's mother-in-law were in the immune response disease process and could resolve it immediately. And, in the case of the nobleman's son, all of this was accomplished at a distance of over 17 miles away! Those who study the immune system know how these processes take time to turn on and off. Administration of a vaccine can take several weeks and may require multiple doses before immunity is achieved. Initiation of targeted drug therapy may take weeks to months to resolve inflammatory cytokines and cell processes before benefits are observed. Even the administration of steroids or antibiotics can take several days to resolve the effects of systemic inflammation or infection.

Many of the immune system's interactions rely on initiating the upregulation of cell proteins, leading to the production of DNA and replication of immune cells. These cells must then travel to the areas of infection and recruit other helper immune cells by creating proteins through DNA and RNA transcription and protein production. In short, to the mortal mind, it takes time to ramp up an immune response, and it also takes time to bring it to a resolution. However, Jesus could somehow fast forward or coordinate all these processes to bring the fever to a prompt resolution.

Spiritual Fever

Like the complexity of the many signals of an immune system, we experience many complex and intertwined human interactions daily. Just as our physical temperature can be raised to purge our bodies of harmful infections, we are subjected to a fiery furnace of adversity, affliction, disappointment, failure, and pain for spiritual benefit. In Isaiah, we read:

> "Behold, I have created the smith that bloweth the coals in the fire, and that bringeth forth an instrument for his work; and I have created the waster to destroy."[3]

Jesus, the Creator, has also created situations where we face hardships. Lehi, a prophet in the Book of Mormon, taught his son Jacob that "there must be an opposition in all things"; otherwise, "righteousness could not be brought to pass."[4] As God's people, "we must be tried in all things"[5] to be prepared to receive blessings in this life and eternal life in the next. The heat of adversity from the refiner's fire can make us more pure, holy, and refined. We can be transformed into a more valuable instrument to bring forth the Lord's work.

The scriptures are replete with the theme of physical heat as an allegory for adversity. Shadrach, Meschach, and Abednego were thrown into a fiery furnace when they refused to pray and worship anything or anyone other than the true and living God. Abinadi was burned at the hand of Noah for not recounting his words that Christ would come down to earth to save His people from their sins. The apostle Peter taught,

> "That the trial of your faith, being much more precious than of gold that perisheth, though it be tried with fire, might be found unto praise and honour and glory at the appearance of Jesus Christ."[6]

Like elevated temperature can signify a battle within our bodies to help keep us healthy and strong, the elevated spiritual temperature of trials, adversity, and affliction can strengthen our spirits. The miracle of the nobleman's son also teaches the way to spiritual healing. He is the way. The Savior is here to assist when we are in the heat of our physical or spiritual adversity or affliction. No matter how far we have distanced ourselves from the Savior for whatever reason, no distance is too great for the prompt and complete healing power of the Savior Jesus Christ. He can provide reassurance that our adversity "shall be but a small moment."[7] He reminds us that He willingly took upon himself the pains and afflictions so that his "bowels would be filled with mercy" so that he might know how to succor us in our infirmities.[8] He reminds us that no matter our burdens if we take His yoke upon us, our burdens may be light.[9]

> 28 Come unto me, all ye that labour and are heavy laden, and I will give you rest.
> 29 Take my yoke upon you, and learn of me; for I am meek and lowly in heart: and ye shall find rest unto your souls.
> 30 For my yoke is easy, and my burden is light

Reflection:
1. How has the Savior helped you during times of adversity or trial?
2. What does it mean to you to come unto the Savior?

3. Prayerfully consider one thing you can do to come unto the Savior so that He can lighten your burdens. Work on this and ponder upon the blessings you see by choosing to turn to him in your trials.

---

[1] John 4:50

[2] Genesis 1:5

[3] Isaiah 54:16

[4] 2 Nephi 2:11

[5] Doctrine and Covenants 136:31

[6] 1 Peter 1:7

[7] Doctrine and Covenants 121:7

[8] Alma 7:11-12

[9] Matthew 11:30

Chapter 3

The Miracle of the Fishes

The call to assist him in the vineyard came with three simple words, "Come, follow me." The account of the Savior calling His apostles is significant enough that it appears in all four of the gospels (Matthew 4:18-24, Mark 1:16-20, Luke 5:1-11, John 1:35-49,). The accounts in Matthew and Mark are very similar. Jesus finds Peter and his brother Andrew mending their nets by the Sea of Galilee and bids them to follow Him. He declares that he would "make them fishers of men." The calling of the two brothers, James and John, in the second boat was also similar.

However, the gospel of John offers a more detailed account leading up to their call. In this account, John notes that Andrew, Peter's brother, was with John the Baptist the day after the Savior was baptized. As Jesus approached them, John the Baptist testified to Andrew, saying, "Behold, the Lamb of God!"[1] Upon hearing this testimony, John and Andrew followed Jesus and dwelt with him. Andrew, after learning and gaining a testimony himself, then searched out Peter, his brother and fishing partner, to tell him that he had "found the Messias, which is being interpreted, the Christ."[2] He brought the Savior to Peter who is then called as one of His disciples after the miracle of the fishes. On the following day, the Savior called Phillip in Galilee. Similar to Andrew, Phillip after gaining a witness himself went and searched out Nathanael and invited him to "come and see."[3]

This calling process illustrates a common pattern in the calling of the disciples and all followers of Jesus Christ. Some obtain a witness of the Savior and then testify and invite others to come and follow Him and his teachings, while others "believe on their" testimony. Both are gifts of the spirit as noted in Doctrine and Covenants 46:13-14:

13 To some it is given by the Holy Ghost to know that Jesus Christ is the Son of God, and that he was crucified for the sins of the world.

14 To others it is given to believe on their words, that they also might have eternal life if they continue faithful.

The account in Luke, however, is perhaps the most profound and well-known. When calling Peter, Andrew, James, and John, the Savior performed a miracle on behalf of the four disciples before inviting them to follow Him. Christ was teaching the people on the shore of the Sea of Galilee as his future disciples were cleaning their nets following an unsuccessful night of fishing. The Savior borrowed Peter's boat to teach the multitude from the shore. After teaching, he told Simon Peter to head to sea and cast out his net again. Reluctantly, Peter complied. So great was the catch of fish that it filled both of the ships and caused the ships to begin to sink. Feeling unworthy of this blessing from the Savior, Peter confessed his unworthiness to the Savior. With words of comfort, the Savior told him to fear not, for he will gather his fellow men from henceforth to the gospel of Christ.

In Luke chapter 5, we read:

1 And it came to pass, that, as the people pressed upon him to hear the word of God, he stood by the lake of Gennesaret,

2 And saw two ships standing by the lake: but the fishermen were gone out of them, and were washing their nets.

3 And he entered into one of the ships, which was Simon's, and prayed him that he would thrust out a little from the land. And he sat down, and taught the people out of the ship.

4 Now when he had left speaking, he said unto Simon, Launch out into the deep, and let down your nets for a draught.

5 And Simon answering said unto him, Master, we have toiled all the night, and have taken nothing: nevertheless at thy word I will let down the net.

6 And when they had this done, they inclosed a great multitude of fishes: and their net brake.

7 And they beckoned unto their partners, which were in the other ship, that they should come and help them. And they came, and filled both the ships, so that they began to sink.

8 When Simon Peter saw it, he fell down at Jesus' knees, saying, Depart from me; for I am a sinful man, O Lord.

9 For he was astonished, and all that were with him, at the draught of the fishes which they had taken:

10 And so was also James, and John, the sons of Zebedee, which were partners with Simon. And Jesus said unto Simon, Fear not; from henceforth thou shalt catch men.

11 And when they had brought their ships to land, they forsook all, and followed him.

The Worth of Catch and the Worth of Souls

On the surface, it may not appear all that miraculous that the Savior asked Peter to cast out his net. Was it by chance he was able to catch fish? However, the magnitude of this miracle can be better appreciated by estimating how many fish the Savior might have brought to the fishermen that morning.

The Sea of Gennesaret and the Sea of Galilee are the same body of water. Throughout history, it has been referred to by many different names, and today, it is known as Lake Kinneret or Kinnereth. It is the lowest freshwater lake in the world. At 700 ft below sea level, it is second only to the Dead Sea as the lowest lake in the world. It is approximately 13 miles long by 8 miles wide and has a maximum depth of about 141 feet. Water enters the lake from underground springs and the Jordan River as it flows from north to south. The body of water provides abundant life and water to this desert region.

The lake water level is closely monitored to ensure it remains adequate (see Figure 1). Too much water and the industries and facilities on the shore can become easily flooded. Too little water and the lake risks irreversible saltwater damage. Because of its low elevation, the weight of the freshwater prevents the underground saltwater springs from seeping out and converting the freshwater into saltwater.

If the water level drops below the level indicated by the black line, it is believed that the weight of the freshwater on top will not be sufficient to hold back the salt water, and the freshwater lake will gradually convert to saltwater.

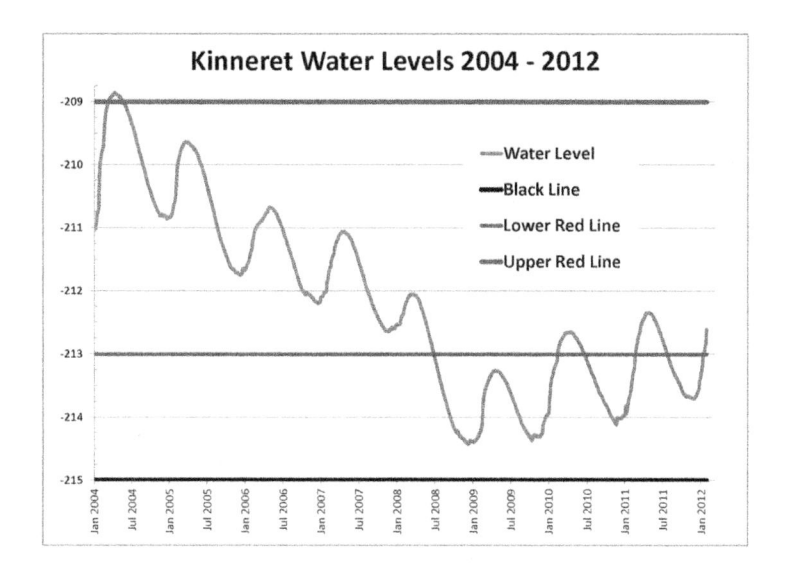

Figure 1.

In the 1980s, the lake faced drought-like conditions and plunged to very low levels, exposing parts of the lake floor. In

1986, a fishing boat was discovered on the northwest shore, later named the Ancient Galilee boat. It was so encased in mud it took 11 years to safely extricate by slowly encasing it in foam for safe removal. According to the Yigal Allon Museum that currently displays the boat, the boat is 27 feet long, 7.5 feet wide, and 4.3 feet deep, with room for about 15 people. Although many refer to the boat as "The Jesus Boat," there is no evidence suggesting this was the very boat Jesus or his disciples used. However, it is widely believed to be from the first century AD based on carbon dating and, therefore, a similar boat used by fishermen of the time. A ship of this size and structure could have been similar to one of the two boats filled with fish from Peter's catch. It is, therefore, possible to estimate how many fish would be required to cause a boat of this size to sink and what the worth of such a catch might be.

William and Rochelle Houser had a similar question in 2017 and published their findings on academia.edu. Although boats can be very heavy (cruise ships, ocean liners, aircraft carriers, etc), they float according to the physics principle of buoyancy. Buoyancy states that the force that keeps the boat floating equals the water the ship displaces. In other words, when the weight of the boat and its cargo exceeds the weight of the water displaced by the boat, the boat will begin to sink. By calculating the weight of the displaced water and subtracting the weight of the boat, one can determine the weight of fish required to cause the boat to start to sink.

The weight of displaced water is the weight of water in cubic feet multiplied by the volume of the boat. Based on the dimensions and shape of the boat reported by the museum, they determined that the volume of the boat is 531.9 cubic feet. Given the weight of water is 62.3 pounds per cubic ft, the weight of water displaced by the boat is 33,137 pounds. Based on an average boat thickness of 2 inches and the fact that most wood during that time was cedar, using the volume of the wood multiplied by the average density of cedar, they estimate the boat to be about 1315 pounds. Factoring in additional weight for cargo and supplies, they calculate the ship could hold up to 31,348 pounds of fish before it would start to sink, putting the catch of 2 boats at a total of 62,696 pounds!

The next question the research team tried to determine was the worth of this catch. Unfortunately, the earliest information regarding commodity pricing is the "Edict of Maximum Prices" in 301 AD. The price for first-quality freshwater fish is 12 Denarii, and second-quality fish is 8 Denarii per libra. A pound equals 454.5 grams, and one libra is 326 grams, making the total catch equal to 87,409 libras. The total catch would be anywhere from about 700,000 to 1.05 Million denarii, depending on determined fish quality. Next, based on the number of days one would work per year and the average salary per day worked, they postulate that catch alone brought in 24-36 years' worth of wages at general laborer rates and 12-18 years' worth of salary at skilled laborer rates for each of the four disciples. They conclude that since modern financial advisers recommend having saved 25 years worth of living expenses to retire, the money obtained from a catch that day (assuming that such an influx of fish at one time wouldn't drive the price of fish down substantially) was sufficient to fund the retirement of each of the 4 fisherman disciples called by Jesus that day.

Thus, we see the worth of the catch and the worth of souls. Jesus called the four fishermen to become fishers of men. He not only called them to follow Him but also very well likely could have provided the financial means to support them and their family so they could leave everything behind and follow him.

Haul of Fishes: Part 2

After Jesus suffered in Gethsemane, was crucified on the cross, laid in a tomb, and rose on the third day, He appeared to his disciples on several occasions. One of those occasions is written in the account of John chapter 21. Once again, the disciples found themselves on the Sea of Tiberias. The ministry of the Savior had been fast, and the disciples were likely discussing where they should go from here with the Savior gone. Peter, reverting to old times, said that he would go fishing, and the others decided to join him.

Despite fishing all night, they caught nothing. As they returned, there was an unfamiliar figure standing on the shore. This unknown figure called out to them, asking if they had caught anything. When they replied no, he suggested they cast their nets on the right side of the ship. Upon doing so, they could not bring the net in because of the greatness of the load. John declares that at this time, they immediately recognized that it was the Lord, which caused Peter to jump out of the ship and swim to shore. As they dined, Jesus gave his famous sermon to his disciples that if they loved him, they should feed his sheep.

Here is the account in John 21:

> 1 After these things Jesus shewed himself again to the disciples at the sea of Tiberias; and on this wise shewed he himself.
> 2 There were together Simon Peter, and Thomas called Didymus, and Nathanael of Cana in Galilee, and the sons of Zebedee, and two other of his disciples.
> 3 Simon Peter saith unto them, I go a fishing. They say unto him, We also go with thee. They went forth, and entered into a ship immediately; and that night they caught nothing.
> 4 But when the morning was now come, Jesus stood on the shore: but the disciples knew not that it was Jesus.
> 5 Then Jesus saith unto them, Children, have ye any meat? They answered him, No.
> 6 And he said unto them, Cast the net on the right side of the ship, and ye shall find. They cast therefore, and now they were not able to draw it for the multitude of fishes.

7 Therefore that disciple whom Jesus loved saith unto Peter, It is the Lord. Now when Simon Peter heard that it was the Lord, he girt his fisher's coat unto him, (for he was naked,) and did cast himself into the sea.

8 And the other disciples came in a little ship; (for they were not far from land, but as it were two hundred cubits,) dragging the net with fishes.

9 As soon then as they were come to land, they saw a fire of coals there, and fish laid thereon, and bread.

10 Jesus saith unto them, Bring of the fish which ye have now caught.

11 Simon Peter went up, and drew the net to land full of great fishes, an hundred and fifty and three: and for all there were so many, yet was not the net broken.

12 Jesus saith unto them, Come and dine. And none of the disciples durst ask him, Who art thou? knowing that it was the Lord.

13 Jesus then cometh, and taketh bread, and giveth them, and fish likewise.

14 This is now the third time that Jesus shewed himself to his disciples, after that he was risen from the dead.

As they sat and dined, the Savior asked Peter three times if he loved him, to which Jesus responded, "Feed my sheep." Elder Jeffrey R. Holland said that the conversation may have continued something perhaps like this:

"Peter, why are you here? Why are we back on this same shore, by these same nets, having this same conversation? Wasn't it obvious then and isn't it obvious now that if I want fish, I can get fish? What I need, Peter, are disciples—and I need them forever. I need someone to feed my sheep and save my lambs. I need someone to preach my gospel and defend my faith. I need someone who loves me, truly, truly loves me, and loves what our Father in Heaven has commissioned me to do. Ours is not a feeble message.

It is not a fleeting task. It is not hapless; it is not hopeless; it is not to be consigned to the ash heap of history. It is the work of Almighty God, and it is to change the world. So, Peter, for the second and presumably the last time, I am asking you to leave all this and to go teach and testify, labor and serve loyally until the day in which they will do to you exactly what they did to me."[4]

Seek ye first the kingdom of God

These two accounts offer a dramatic example of a lifelong principle of the gospel. The Savior taught it himself in the Sermon on the Mount. Instead of worrying about our temporal cares of life and things even considered to be necessities - food, clothing, shelter - he counsels us to "seek ye first the kingdom of God, and his righteousness; and all these things shall be added unto you."[5] If the work and glory of God are to bring to pass the immortality and eternal life of man[6], then this should become our primary work and our glory, too. He doesn't want us to be fishers of fish. He wants us to become fishers of men.

The Book of Mormon further emphasizes the importance of putting God first. The prophet Jacob elaborates that we should first seek God, but if we are blessed with wealth, it should be used to bless the lives of others.

> "But before ye seek for riches, seek ye for the kingdom of God. And after ye have obtained a hope in Christ ye shall obtain riches, if ye seek them; and ye will seek them for the intent to do good—to clothe the naked, and to feed the hungry, and to liberate the captive, and administer relief to the sick and the afflicted."[7]

The Lord was also clear in establishing his priorities for the early laborers restoring His gospel. When Oliver Cowdery,

Hyrum Smith, and Joseph Knight came to the prophet seeking a revelation regarding their role to bring forth the restoration of the gospel, the Savior, through the prophet Joseph Smith, told them to "keep my commandments and to seek to bring forth and establish the cause of Zion." Additionally, Oliver and Hyrum were admonished to not seek after riches but for wisdom. They were told the mysteries of God leading to eternal life would make them rich.

Words to Oliver Cowdrey (D&C 6:6-7), to Hyrum Smith (D&C 11:6-7), Joseph Knight, Sr (D&C 12:6) read,

> "Now, as you have asked, behold, I say unto you, keep my commandments, and seek to bring forth and establish the cause of Zion; Seek not for riches but for wisdom, and behold, the mysteries of God shall be unfolded unto you, and then shall you be made rich. Behold, he that hath eternal life is rich."

I gained an understanding of this gospel principle early on in my life as a college and medical school student. When I returned home from my mission in Japan and returned to BYU as a sophomore, I thought I should pursue a career in medicine. It was critical to do well in my core sciences classes to obtain the necessary grades for medical schools to even consider me an applicant and to learn the material well enough to receive a qualifying score on the Medical College Admission Test (MCAT). This meant countless hours studying for classes and exams while I worked a part-time job to help support our new young family.

Early on, much like Oliver, Hyrum, and Joseph Knight, I sought the Lord in prayer, seeking guidance as to how I could succeed. The impression came specific and unique to me: keep the Sabbath Day holy by not studying on Sunday. I followed this impression and was fortunate to do well in my classes and well enough on the MCAT. With the Lord's help, I was eventually admitted to multiple medical schools and chose to attend the University of Vermont. I soon learned firsthand just how difficult and demanding medical school could be. Starting as a parent of one child, I soon transformed into a parent of three. With additional opportunities to provide meaningful service in the community and at church, there never seemed to be enough time. We had significant exams spanning multiple topics of medicine that occurred nearly every week and always first thing Monday morning. How was I to succeed if I could not study and review the material from the week on Sunday?

Relying on my impressions in college, I decided to proceed with faith and to follow the personal commandment of the Spirit when I asked the Lord for his help. Rather than studying on Sunday, I decided to study all day Saturday, eat dinner with my family, spend time with the kids in the evening, and then, after putting them to bed, study again until midnight Saturday night. To make final preparations for the Monday morning exam, I went to bed early Sunday evening and woke up early Monday morning to study for a few hours before classes. On multiple occasions, as I reviewed the material one last time Monday morning, I felt guided by the spirit to review certain points of the material.

For me, taking the Monday morning exams often became a spiritual experience. Impressions came into my mind of how I should answer the questions. On multiple occasions, I was led to review particular points that appeared on the test. Often, I felt the reassurance from the Holy Ghost that the wisdom I was being blessed with was a direct consequence of my desire to seek first the kingdom of God and act on the impressions I received guiding me personally on how I should do so.

The Savior desires all of God's children to come unto Him. He desires to be a part of our lives, to help and support us. I love the image of the painting of the Savior knocking on the outside of the door. It has been described as a door with no knob on the outside. Although He may knock, we must open the door and welcome Him into our lives. We have to come unto Jesus.

"Behold, I stand at the door, and knock: if any man hear my voice, and open the door, I will come in to him, and will sup with him, and he with me."[8]

Although his disciples had returned to old ways, the Savior once again appeared on the shore, and they came unto Him. As they spent time with him, felt his love, and declared their love for Him, he gently reminded them of their work and glory. Likewise, once we are converted, our role is to strengthen those around us.[9] Our life's mission is to feed His sheep.

Reflection:
1. What blessings have you seen in your life by putting the Savior and his gospel at the center of your life?
2. How can paying a full tithing and a generous fast offering open the windows of heaven in your life?
3. Prayerfully invite the Holy Ghost to teach you what you can start doing or stop doing so that you more fully seek the kingdom of God.

---

[1] John 1:36

[2] John 1:41

[3] John 1:46

[4] Jeffrey R. Holland. "The First Great Commandment". General Conference, October 2012

[5] Matthew 6:33

[6] Moses 1:39

[7] Jacob 2:18-19

[8] Revelations 3:20.

[9] Luke 22:32

Chapter 4

Jesus Casts out Evil Spirits

As Jesus continued calling His disciples on the shores of Galilee, the Savior traveled northward along the sea to Capernaum. The Savior entered the synagogue on the Sabbath day not only to worship but to "teach as one who had authority, and not as the scribes."[1] On this occasion, His disciples learn that His power and authority extend not only to the physical, such as finding fish and fixing fevers, but also to the spiritual.

The first detailed account of Jesus' power over spirits occurs in both Mark chapter 1 and Luke chapter 4. The accounts are very similar. While in the synagogue Jesus meets a man possessed with an unclean spirit. The unclean spirit recognizes Jesus as the Son of God and pleads to be left alone. Both record that by the Savior's word, the unclean spirit is cast out of the man to the astonishment of the witnesses in the synagogue. The accounts differ, however, in how the spirit is described. Mark refers to the spirit as an "unclean spirit"[2] whereas Luke describes it as a "spirit of an unclean devil."[3] Furthermore, after the spirit is rebuked, Mark states that "the unclean spirit had torn him,"[4] suggesting that perhaps the man was injured by the spirit. Luke's account seems to clarify that after being rebuked, the devil "came out of him, and hurt him not."[5] The following is the account in the book of Mark.

> 23 And there was in their synagogue a man with an unclean spirit; and he cried out,
> 24 Saying, Let us alone; what have we to do with thee, thou Jesus of Nazareth? art thou come to destroy us? I know thee who thou art, the Holy One of God.
> 25 And Jesus rebuked him, saying, Hold thy peace, and come out of him.

> 26 And when the unclean spirit had torn him, and cried with a loud voice, he came out of him.
>
> 27 And they were all amazed, insomuch that they questioned among themselves, saying, What thing is this? what new doctrine is this? For with authority commandeth he even the unclean spirits, and they do obey him.
>
> 28 And immediately his fame spread abroad throughout all the region round about Galilee.

Though Jesus had demonstrated power over the things in the physical world, Jesus was now demonstrating his power over the spiritual world. For those present, witnessing Jesus's ability to command darkness and evil out of this poor man must have been truly remarkable. As stated, "they were all amazed" and questioned themselves saying, "What thing is this?". How could Jesus, whom they saw as a mere man coming out of Nazareth, command the darkness to leave this man? What gave him such authority that even the evil spirits had to obey?

His power over evil spirits was demonstrated an additional five times and is the most frequent miracle performed by the Savior. The second account of Jesus' power over evil spirits was when he cast out many spirits in a man. This is documented in Mark 5:1-20, Luke 8:26-29, and Matthew 8:28-34. Matthew describes two men who were possessed of devils and were so tormented that they prevented people from passing by the way in the country of Gergesenes, whereas Mark and Luke only mention one man. Additionally, Mark and Luke explain that this man was so tormented that he could not live anywhere but in tombs, and despite attempts to restrain him with chains, he would break them and would cry day and night cutting himself with stones. Before casting out the evil spirit named Legion, meaning many, all three accounts indicate that the evil spirits were so desperate to experience a physical body that they pleaded with Jesus to allow them to enter a nearby herd of swine. Upon doing so, the swine violently fled off the side of a cliff to their demise. This event was so disturbing that the whole city came out to meet Jesus and asked him to depart.

> 28 And when he was come to the other side into the country of the Gergesenes, there met him two possessed with devils, coming out of the tombs, exceeding fierce, so that no man might pass by that way.
> 29 And, behold, they cried out, saying, What have we to do with thee, Jesus, thou Son of God? art thou come hither to torment us before the time?
> 30 And there was a good way off from them an herd of many swine feeding.
> 31 So the devils besought him, saying, If thou cast us out, suffer us to go away into the herd of swine.
> 32 And he said unto them, Go. And when they were come out, they went into the herd of swine: and, behold, the whole herd of swine ran violently down a steep place into the sea, and perished in the waters.
> 33 And they that kept them fled, and went their ways into the city, and told every thing, and what was befallen to the possessed of the devils.
> 34 And, behold, the whole city came out to meet Jesus: and when they saw him, they besought him that he would depart out of their coasts.

The third account is exclusively in Matthew 9. After Jesus healed two blind men, a man unable to speak was brought to Jesus. Once the devil was cast out, he could speak again, and the people marveled.

> 32 As they went out, behold, they brought to him a dumb man possessed with a devil.

> 33 And when the devil was cast out, the dumb spake: and the multitudes marvelled, saying, It was never so seen in Israel.

The fourth account is detailed in Matthew 12:22-37, Mark 3:20-30, and Luke 11:14-26. Matthew describes the man as unable to see or speak, whereas Mark only mentions that he can not speak. Luke doesn't focus on the man or the casting out of the devil and instead focuses on the discussion raised by the Pharisees regarding what power this could be accomplished. Jesus knew the thoughts of the Pharisees who were discussing and thinking among themselves that he was using Satan's power to perform the miracle. He rebukes them saying that would be the same as a house or kingdom divided against itself and that a house or kingdom divided against itself cannot stand. In Matthew chapter 12, we read:

> 22 Then was brought unto him one possessed with a devil, blind, and dumb: and he healed him, insomuch that the blind and dumb both spake and saw.
> 23 And all the people were amazed, and said, Is not this the son of David?
> 24 But when the Pharisees heard it, they said, This fellow doth not cast out devils, but by Beelzebub the prince of the devils.
> 25 And Jesus knew their thoughts, and said unto them, Every kingdom divided against itself is brought to desolation; and every city or house divided against itself shall not stand:
> 26 And if Satan cast out Satan, he is divided against himself; how shall then his kingdom stand?
> 27 And if I by Beelzebub cast out devils, by whom do your children cast them out? therefore they shall be your judges.
> 28 But if I cast out devils by the Spirit of God, then the kingdom of God is come unto you.

In Matthew 15:21-28 and Mark 7:24-30, there is an account of a Canaanite woman who requested that the Savior cast out a devil from her daughter. The account in Matthew is rather different from other casting out of Spirits because Jesus initially would not talk to her. He likely asked His disciples to send her away because she was not of the house of Israel, which the Savior was called to minister to first. However, she persisted and came unto Him again and demonstrated great enough faith that He healed her daughter.

> 22 And, behold, a woman of Canaan came out of the same coasts, and cried unto him, saying, Have mercy on me, O Lord, thou Son of David; my daughter is grievously vexed with a devil.
> 23 But he answered her not a word. And his disciples came and besought him, saying, Send her away; for she crieth after us.
> 24 But he answered and said, I am not sent but unto the lost sheep of the house of Israel.
> 25 Then came she and worshipped him, saying, Lord, help me.
> 26 But he answered and said, It is not meet to take the children's bread, and to cast it to dogs.
> 27 And she said, Truth, Lord: yet the dogs eat of the crumbs which fall from their masters' table.
> 28 Then Jesus answered and said unto her, O woman, great is thy faith: be it unto thee even as thou wilt. And her daughter was made whole from that very hour.

The final account of Jesus casting out evil spirits occurs in Matthew 17:14-21 and is also described in Mark 9:14-29 and Luke 9:37-43. A man brings his son to the Savior and states that he is possessed by an evil spirit that forces him to fall into the water or hot coals resulting in damage to his body. He first went to Jesus' disciples but they could not cast out the devil.

Faith and belief become the subject of Jesus' discourse before performing the miracle. The account in Mark is unique. Before casting out the devil, Jesus tells the boy's father that "all things are possible to him that believeth."[6] The Father responds by saying, "Lord, I believe; help thou my unbelief."[7]

Although the focus of faith and belief centers on the father in this tender exchange wherein the boy's father requests extra belief from Jesus, the Matthew and Luke accounts seem to focus on Jesus' disciples' lack of faith to perform the miracle. Jesus teaches His disciples that the power to cast out devils is cultivated by faith as small as a mustard seed that can only grow in power through prayer and fasting. Here is the account in Matthew 17:14-21.

> 14 And when they were come to the multitude, there came to him a certain man, kneeling down to him, and saying,
> 15 Lord, have mercy on my son: for he is lunatic, and sore vexed: for ofttimes he falleth into the fire, and oft into the water.
> 16 And I brought him to thy disciples, and they could not cure him.
> 17 Then Jesus answered and said, O faithless and perverse generation, how long shall I be with you? how long shall I suffer you? bring him hither to me.
> 18 And Jesus rebuked the devil; and he departed out of him: and the child was cured from that very hour.
> 19 Then came the disciples to Jesus apart, and said, Why could not we cast him out?
> 20 And Jesus said unto them, Because of your unbelief: for verily I say unto you, If ye have faith as a grain of mustard seed, ye shall say unto this mountain, Remove hence to yonder place; and it shall remove; and nothing shall be impossible unto you.
> 21 Howbeit this kind goeth not out but by prayer and fasting.

Jesus: the Light of the World

Jesus Christ is the light of the world. He declares, "I am the light of the world: he that followeth me shall not walk in darkness, but shall have the light of life."[8] As the creator of the world, He said, "Let there be light: and there was light."[9] Through these words, he "divided the light from the darkness" during the first day of the creation.[10] He is "the light which shineth...which light proceedeth forth from the presence of God to fill the immensity of space."[11] It is His light that, therefore, replaces the darkness in the universe. Indeed, "God is light, and in him there is no darkness at all."[12] It is the light of Jesus Christ "which is in all things, which giveth life to all things."[13]

Just as the opposite of light is darkness, the antithesis to the Savior and His light is Lucifer, the fallen angel, and all of those spirits who follow him. His objective is to "spread the works of darkness" over the face of the earth.[14] He is the master deceiver and counterfeiter who tries to "put darkness for light, and light for darkness" to "call evil good, and good evil."[15] However, because Jesus IS "the light which shineth in the darkness,"[16] Sharon Eubank explains, "that means no matter how hard it tries, the darkness cannot put out that light. Ever. You can trust that His light will be there for you."[17]

When the Savior spoke the words, "Hold thy peace, and come out of Him" the unclean devil spirit had no other choice but to comply. It is a spiritual law governing the universe. "That which doth not edify is not of God, and is darkness."[18] Just as light rebukes darkness in the physical sense, Jesus Christ, as the light and life of the world, has the power to rebuke darkness in the spiritual sense. To understand the power of His light, it is crucial to learn more about what we know regarding the properties of light.

What is light?

Flip on a switch as you enter a dark room. Instantly the light is turned on, the room is illuminated, and you can see the objects in the room. Though light may appear as simple as an on/off switch, entire textbooks and several branches of physics are devoted to this very question: what is light? On one hand, light can be defined as a particle. A small, finite object known as a photon. As a particle, this photon has a position in the universe. It has momentum and direction as it travels through space. However, because its resting mass is zero, photon particles differ from traditional matter. On the other hand, light can also be defined as and behave like a wave. Waves, unlike distinct particles, can travel through or around objects. Waves can interfere, cancel, or magnify one another. They are not localized to a particular position like a particle, but they may transfer energy or information from one location to another.

To help understand the differences between particles and waves, consider yourself an ocean swimmer far from shore. You behave like a particle; you have a position in the water, and swim in a direction. Despite rocking up and down as the waves move by, the individual water molecules around you also behave like particles as they move up and down together with you as you float. However, ocean water as a whole may be characterized as a wave. The ocean waves, as they move up and down, are transferring energy horizontally from the sea to the shore. This energy propagates through the waves even though the individual water particles may stay right next to you as they bob up and down.

The unique nature of light behaving like a particle and wave gave rise to the branch of physics called quantum mechanics. The term that describes light as both a particle and a wave is called wave-particle duality. The basic premise is that light, and every other material in the universe may be at times best described and defined as a particle, whereas other times it is best described and defined as a wave.

As we consider light to behave like a wave, most of us are familiar with light discernible by our eye on the visible spectrum as light waves. Visible light is a form of electromagnetic radiation - oscillating wavelengths of energy - that produces light waves visible to the human eye. Waves are characterized by amplitude, the height of each wave crest, wavelength, and the distance required for the wave to repeat from crest to crest. According to the wave model of light, the amplitude determines the intensity of the light, whereas the wavelength determines the nature of the light or, in the case of visible light, the color of that light. Light waves with a longer wavelength have fewer waves over a given period of time and, therefore, a lower frequency, whereas light waves with shorter wavelengths have more wave cycles in a given period of time and, therefore, have a higher frequency.

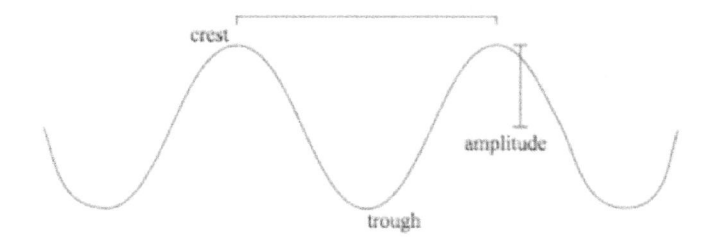

Electromagnetic radiation can range from low-frequency radio or microwaves that have wavelengths as long as many meters (i.e. long, rolling, calm waves in the ocean), to high-frequency radiation waves such as ultraviolet, x-ray, or gamma rays as short as .0001 nanometers that can cause or treat cancer (i.e short powerful breaking waves on the shore).

Visible light is a narrow band of electromagnetic radiation that ranges between 400 nanometers for violet light and 700 nanometers for red light. The size of the wavelength will determine what color an object is. When light hits a "red" object, it reflects a wavelength of 650 nm back to our eye and the image appears red. Objects that appear as red absorb all of the other wavelengths of the visible light spectrum but reflect back the 650 nm length waves, the wavelength of the color red. White light contains all wavelengths, and when reflected through the glass of a prism, the different wavelengths can be separated, and a rainbow can appear. Even in the dark of the night, living creatures emit electromagnetic radiation light energy below the visible spectrum that can be visualized using infrared goggles. Light truly gives life to the world. Any object that isn't at absolute zero in temperature emits detectable light. This light is released energy from the movement of atoms and given that Christ is the light of the world, he is the source of this energy in all things.

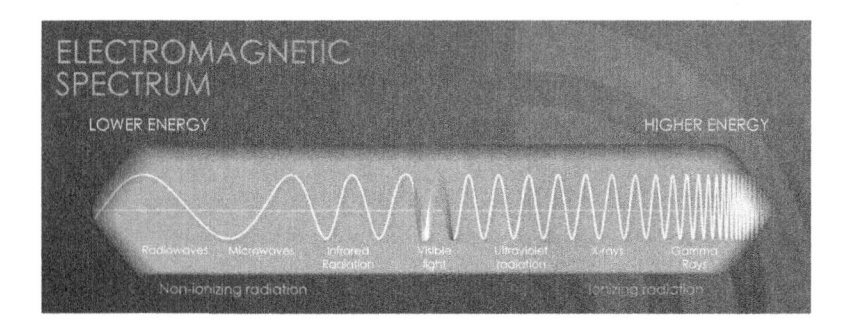

Albert Einstein won a Nobel prize for his experiments that helped prove that light could also behave as discrete particles of energy and is credited for the term photons. He observed that when metal was exposed to a wavelength of light energy above a certain threshold, electrons, called photoelectrons, could be measured flowing out of the material. Increasing the frequency of the applied light wave, however, did not lead to an increase in the number of particles being emitted. Instead, increasing the frequency increased the kinetic energy of the emitted photoelectron. When the amplitude of the applied light wave was increased, it did not increase the kinetic energy of the ejected particle. An increase in amplitude instead increased the number of ejected photoelectrons measured by an increase in current. In summary, he found that amplitude determined the number of ejected particles and frequency determined the energy of those ejected particles. This was a revolutionary finding.

To understand how one would have expected light to behave in the framework of the wave theory instead of Einstein's particle theory, consider the following tennis analogy. A tennis ball is like a particle. When you increase the frequency of hitting you have more balls bouncing back at you over a given period of time. If you increase the intensity of the hit then the ball will bounce back at you with more strength. However, if the tennis ball is a wave, Einstein postulated that increasing the frequency would increase the energy of the ball coming back off the wall, and increasing the amplitude would increase the number of balls that would bounce back at you.

And this is what Einstein observed. Increasing the frequency of the applied light to the metal increased the kinetic energy of the emitted photoelectron, and increasing the amplitude of the applied light increased the number of emitted photoelectrons (current).

A particle of light with a higher frequency has more kinetic energy (energy of motion). A faster tennis ball, though a particle, has more kinetic energy, and therefore, the ball, when it bounces off the wall, has more kinetic energy. The intensity of the applied light wave, or in other words increased amplitude, instead should be likened to throwing more than one ball at the same time with a certain kinetic energy. If multiple balls are thrown at a wall simultaneously, then multiple balls are observed bouncing off the wall. The more balls pitched (i.e., increased amplitude), the more balls bounce off a wall (known as current) at a certain level of kinetic energy. With light, the greater amplitude of light leads to a brighter or greater light intensity at a certain wavelength. If the frequency of light emitted is 6.66×10^{14} hz, corresponding to the wavelength of 450 nm, then it would appear blue. Increasing the amplitude of this frequency would make the blue light appear brighter or more intense. Let's explore how the laws of the frequency and intensity of light can relate to the spiritual light within us.

Let His Light So Shine

On a memorable weekend with the local scout troop, we traveled to an area called the Lava Tubes outside of Meadow, Utah. Tucked in the ground of a rather unassuming flat and dusty desert surface are three tunnels formed out of lava rock. We ventured into the depths of one of the caves to set up our sleeping arrangements. As the sun's glow dipped over the horizon, bringing a blanket of darkness over both entrances to each of the caves, it soon became clear how valuable our flashlights and headlamps would be. As we gathered in a circle before our evening prayer, I shared a Scoutmaster's Minute. I asked each scout to place their fingers on the buttons of their headlamps or flashlights. On the count of three, we all turned off our lights.

Immediately we were engulfed by the thick darkness. There was not one speck of visible light to be seen. None of us had been in anything so absent of light. I shared that this is what life would be without Jesus Christ because He is the light of the world. I asked one of the scouts to turn on his light. The small light immediately chased away the darkness and the contours of the cave walls could be seen. One by one figures and objects could begin to be discernible as we slowly turned the lights back on. With time individual faces could soon be recognized until the light grew and grew as it chased away the darkness around us.

So it is with the light of Christ. But, only if we invite Jesus Christ into our life. By following His commandments and doing His will, we are filled with His light. "He that keepeth his commandments receiveth truth and light,"[19] and does so "line upon line, precept upon precept, here a little, and there a little,"[20] His light can grow within us "brighter and brighter until that perfect day."[21] Just as metal exposed to increasing frequencies of light emits photoelectrons with increasing energy, and increasing the amplitude or intensity of the applied light leads to the increased number of particles emitted, similar effects can be observed in our personal lives when we choose to apply Christ's light.

His gospel, love, grace, and atonement can inject life and energy into our minds, hearts, and spirits. We can be awakened from spiritual darkness. As we yearn for and step into His light, the light of Christ can rebuke the unclean tendencies that may exist in our natures. The more frequently we walk in His light - the more exposure to Christ's light in a given time period - the greater influence He can have on us. This increased frequency leads to a higher energy and a greater power to change our natures. It increases our ability to move past the threshold of our natural man tendencies and launch to a higher plane of spirituality. It gives us the kinetic energy, the energy of motion, to overcome the inertia required to change and make choices that will put off the natural man and allow us to become a saint through the atonement of Jesus Christ.[22] It gives us the energy to consistently choose faith and the covenant path when things become challenging.

The more **inten**tly we seek his influence, just like increasing the **inten**sity or amplitude of the influence of Christ's light in our life, the more measured opportunities and experiences we can have bringing people to Christ. When we intently fill our life with his light, we increase our ability to reflect His light to others. We can more fully follow his admonition to "Let your light so shine before me, that they may see your good works, and glorify your Father which is in heaven."[23] In his message to the Nephites, the Savior clarified and emphasized that "I am the light which ye shall hold up - that which ye have seen me do."[24]

I was able to experience firsthand how applying the light of Christ with increased frequency and intensity was able to invoke changes in people's lives as a missionary for the Church of Jesus Christ in Japan. My companion and I met a man walking a scrappy, malnourished dog down the street. The man was sad and had a dull countenance. We began teaching him the gospel in the final weeks of my mission. He finished the missionary lessons and committed to baptism during the week I traveled around Japan with my parents before returning to the United States. To my joy, I witnessed his baptism before flying home. Although I had seen him nearly daily just a week prior, I was astonished at the change in his appearance during the week that had passed since I had last seen him. By committing to following the Savior, repenting, and inviting the light of Christ to influence every part of his being, Brother Sugano had received the image of the Savior in his countenance and his face was radiant. I almost didn't recognize him. To me, it seemed as if he was transformed like the people of Nephi who were praying to the Savior during the account of his visitation to them.

> "And it came to pass that Jesus blessed them as they did pray unto him; and his countenance did smile upon them, and the **light** of his countenance did **shine** upon them, and behold they were as white as the countenance and also the garments of Jesus; and behold the whiteness thereof did exceed all the whiteness, yea, even there could be nothing upon earth so white as the whiteness thereof."[25]

When we make room for the Savior in our life and allow for the energy of His light to fill our life, we allow His light to bring us to a higher plane of energy and we can emit a greater intensity of light from our countenances - His light! Alma, the younger, clearly understood this concept as he pleaded to the church in Zarahemla. He said,

> "And now behold, I ask of you, my brethren of the church, have ye spiritually been born of God? Have ye received his image in your countenances? Have ye experienced this mighty change in your hearts?"[26]

"I say unto you, can ye look up to God at that day with a pure heart and clean hands? I say unto you, can you look up, having the image of God engraven upon your countenances?"[27]

"And now behold, I say unto you, my brethren, if ye have experienced a change of heart, and if ye have felt to sing the song of redeeming love, I would ask, can ye feel so now?"[28]

It is never too late to choose to receive more of the Savior's light.

Reflection:
1. What is the relationship between obedience, knowledge, and light?
2. What changes can I make to increase Christ's light in my life?
3. How can I more fully share the light of Christ I receive with others?

---

[1] Mark 1:22

[2] Luke 1:23

[3] Luke 4:33

[4] Mark 1:26

[5] Luke 4:33

[6] Mark 9:23

[7] Mark 9:24

[8] John 8:12

[9] Genesis 1:3

[10] Genesis 1:4

[11] Doctrine and Covenants 88:11-12

[12] 1 John 1:5

[13] Doctrine and Covenants 88:13

[14] Helaman 6:28

[15] Isaiah 5:20

[16] D&C 6:21

[17] Sharon Eubank. "Christ: the Light that Shineth in the Darkness." General Conference, April 2019

[18] Doctrine and Covenants 50:23

[19] Doctrine and Covenants 97:28

[20] 2 Nephi 28:20

[21] Doctrine and Covenants 50:24

[22] Mosiah 3:19

[23] Matthew 5:16

[24] 3 Nephi 18:24

[25] 3 Nephi 19:25 (emphasis added)

[26] Alma 5:14

[27] Alma 5:19

[28] Alma 5:26

Chapter 5

Jesus Heals a Leper

By now it was clear to the followers of Jesus that he had the power to heal. Following the casting out of evil spirits and the healing of the sick and the afflicted, throngs of people began flocking to the Savior. After witnessing healings in the synagogue and the healing of Peter's mother-in-law, the scriptures describe that "all the city was gathered together at the door."[1] Jesus healed "divers diseases" and "cast out many devils" and continued to do so from town to town throughout all of Galilee. Indeed, Matthew reports that his fame went throughout all of Syria.[2]

Although society had no limitations preventing the febrile, the lame, or the blind from interacting with the Savior, clear rules were established to separate people who suffered from the disease leprosy. Two chapters of scripture are entirely devoted to recognizing, diagnosing, and treating leprosy.[3] In an algorithmic fashion, it outlines how the priests are to handle people sickened with this disease. For example, several verses are dedicated to the assessment of hair color, skin color, brightness or darkness, and depth of the skin lesions in question.

Why were priests given such a task? To the ancient Jews, leprosy was not simply a disease of the flesh but was viewed as the outward manifestation of the destructive influence that sin can have on a person. The leper was not simply considered sick. They were regarded as sinners and, therefore, pronounced unclean by the priest. Furthermore, the afflicted individual was also required to cry out to the people that they were "unclean, unclean."[4]

Those with leprosy were banished to live in outskirt encampments for the rest of their life. Before their departure, they were required to remove all their clothing for inspection by the priests. After a period of time and ritual washing, the worn garment was, at times, even burned to ashes. In this context, it likely was deeply concerning to Jesus' disciples when the leper approached the Savior to be healed. The following account comes from the first chapter in the book of Mark 1:40-45, although the account also exists in Matthew 8:1-4, and Luke 5:12-15. In Mark, we read:

> 40 And there came a leper to him, beseeching him, and kneeling down to him, and saying unto him, If thou wilt, thou canst make me clean.
> 41 And Jesus, moved with compassion, put forth his hand, and touched him, and saith unto him, I will; be thou clean.
> 42 And as soon as he had spoken, immediately the leprosy departed from him, and he was cleansed.
> 43 And he straitly charged him, and forthwith sent him away;
> 44 And saith unto him, See thou say nothing to any man: but go thy way, shew thyself to the priest, and offer for thy cleansing those things which Moses commanded, for a testimony unto them.
> 45 But he went out, and began to publish it much, and to blaze abroad the matter, insomuch that Jesus could no more openly enter into the city, but was without in desert places: and they came to him from every quarter.

Later in Luke, chapter 17, Jesus healed ten lepers that besought Him to be healed. In contrast to when Jesus healed the one, these ten called out to him from afar asking to be healed, an apparent acknowledgment of established rules separating those with leprosy. Jesus told them to go to the priests and they would be healed. Of note, only one returned to the Savior's to give thanks. As Luke points out the one who returned to give thanks was a Samaritan, a people who were despised by the Jews.

11 And it came to pass, as he went to Jerusalem, that he passed through the midst of Samaria and Galilee.

12 And as he entered into a certain village, there met him ten men that were lepers, which stood afar off:

13 And they lifted up their voices, and said, Jesus, Master, have mercy on us.

14 And when he saw them, he said unto them, Go shew yourselves unto the priests. And it came to pass, that, as they went, they were cleansed.

15 And one of them, when he saw that he was healed, turned back, and with a loud voice glorified God,

16 And fell down on his face at his feet, giving him thanks: and he was a Samaritan.

17 And Jesus answering said, Were there not ten cleansed? but where are the nine?

18 There are not found that returned to give glory to God, save this stranger.

19 And he said unto him, Arise, go thy way: thy faith hath made thee whole.

The Miracle of Skin

Our skin, otherwise known as the integumentary system, is considered the largest organ of the human body and perhaps one of the most overlooked and underappreciated. It protects the inside of our body from external threats such as bacteria, sun, water, and other hazardous chemicals. It not only cushions us from blows, falls, or trauma, but it also can repair itself when such damages occur. It regulates our body temperature so that we don't get too hot or too cold, allowing our internal systems to function at a near-constant temperature. Although most of what is visible to our eye are dead skin cells on the surface, the skin organ is actively alive and can be categorized into three main layers: the epidermis, dermis, and hypodermis.

The outermost epidermal layer provides a waterproof barrier and houses melanocytes that produce varying amounts of melanin that give our skin its tone. The epidermis can be further subdivided into 5 layers, all in varying stages of cell development that give the skin's outer layer its protective elements.

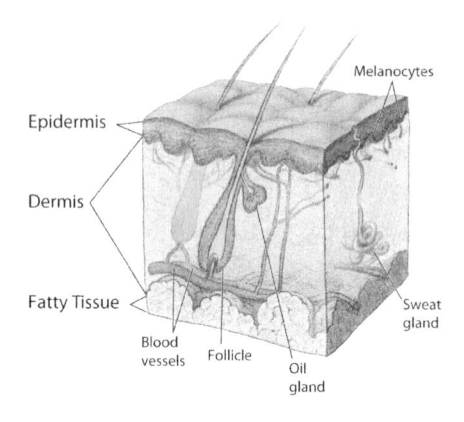

The dermal layer provides strength and stretch to our skin with its abundance of tough yet flexible connective tissue. It contains hair follicles and sweat glands that help regulate body temperature. It houses nerve endings such as mechanoreceptors that provide the sense of touch, thermoreceptors for heat, and nociceptors for the perception of pain. Capillary blood vessels move nutrients in and out of the skin and can dilate or constrict to retain or give off heat. Additionally, the dermis contains the lymphatic system that constantly samples the outside environment and supports the immune system against bacterial invasion.

The hypodermis, or subcutaneous tissue, connects the skin to the underlying muscle or bone. It also contains specialized mechanoreceptors called Pacinian Corpuscles that are especially sensitive to vibrations and can conduct vibrations along the bones of the body.

Given the many layers of skin and its surrounding complexity, it is not surprising that several diseases and conditions affect this organ. From itchy dermatitis such as psoriasis, eczema, dandruff, hives, or rashes, to bacterial infections such as an abscess or cellulitis, or fungal infections such as ringworm or candida, to plugged up sweat glands or pores leading to acne, or cancers such as melanoma, basal cell, or squamous cell, the list of potential ailments of the skin seems never-ending. Much of what we understand about these different types of skin conditions is a result of being able to examine the different cell layers under a microscope - a miracle tool that allows for the diagnosis and treatment of disease by pathologists on a single cellular level. Different cell structures take on various stains in different patterns and can be categorized and distinguished by how they appear after being stained under the light of a microscope.

Leprosy

Leprosy is an infectious disease that has plagued humankind for thousands of years. Throughout civilization, it has often been misunderstood. Some cultures believed it was a hereditary disease, while others claimed it was brought on by sin and, therefore, a curse from God. Before its biological origin as an infectious disease caused by Mycobacterium Leprae was discovered by the Norwegian Dr. Hansen in 1873, treatment was mostly palliative and symptom management. Despite current knowledge of treatment, many of those who contract the disease today are still cast out to leper colonies due to fear.

The disease usually spreads through contact with the infected individuals' respiratory secretions (cough or sneezing). However, transmissibility is fairly low; only 5% of those who contract the mycobacterium go on to develop the disease. For the few who become infected, it may take anywhere from one to twenty years before disease symptoms emerge, the average onset time being five years. The bacteria initially attacks the nerves, typically the small sensory receptors located in the skin. The ensuing nerve damage results in an inability to sense heat or painful touch and the loss of these protective mechanisms can lead to further damage to the skin. Other nerves that control muscle functions may also be affected, leading to contracture deformities of the hands or feet. Openings in the damaged skin lead to secondary bacterial infections that fester unnoticed until they turn into visible sores. If untreated, the damage done to nerves is usually permanent. However, with multi-drug antibiotic therapy treatment can be very effective. People are no longer infectious after one month of treatment and cured after six to twelve months.

The approach to cleansing in biblical times was more complex than simply taking antibiotic medications for an extended period. It was an eight-day ritual. In addition to washing and shaving off all the hair of the affected person, a bird was killed in a pot of running water, and another living bird along with hyssop (minty tree), scarlet, and cedar was dipped in the blood of the killed bird by the priest then sprinkled on the person who was to be cleansed at a total of seven times. The living bird was then set free.[5] On the eighth day, a sacrifice of an unblemished young lamb, oil, and flour is made to pronounce the affected clean.

Touch of the Master's Hand

Jesus' method of healing and cleansing the one leper who dared to approach Him was entirely different from how he healed the ten lepers in Luke. Being moved with compassion by the word of his mouth and, perhaps even more importantly, first the touch of His hand, the Savior pronounced the man with leprosy clean. In His previous miracles, the Savior had simply spoken and it was done. He told the servants of Mary to draw wine from water jugs to serve the banquet guests. He simply spoke to the nobleman "Go thy way, thy son liveth" when he cured his son of a distant fever. He told Simon to put down his nets again to draw up fish. He rebuked the evil spirits by simply speaking the words "come out." Even the ten lepers were healed after following his spoken word. But this time was different. It was up close. It was personal. It was preceded by the Savior's touch. And this meant everything to the leper.

George MacDonald, a 19th-century Scottish writer and minister explains the importance of the Savior's touch in this healing miracle:

> "Jesus could have cured him with a word. There was no need He should touch him. No need did I say? There was every need. For no one else would touch him. The healthy human hand, always more or less healing, was never laid on him; he was despised and rejected. It was a poor thing for the Lord to cure his body; he must comfort and cure his sore heart. Of all men a leper, I say, needed to be touched with the hand of love...It was not for our master, our brother, our ideal man, to draw around him the skirts of his garments and speak a lofty word of healing, that the man might at least be clean before he touched him. The man was his brother, and an evil disease cleaved fast unto him...I thank God that the touch went before the word...That touch was more than the healing."[6]

Just like our skin is a miracle organ that protects our bodies from damage and outside influences, we need similar protection for our spirits. Our skin has the innate power to protect and repair, but through the Savior's power, this was unlocked in the man with leprosy. Through the touch of the Savior and His power, the wounds of the leper were bound up, healed, and repaired.

There are four simple building blocks from which all cells, tissues, and organs are physically created. The four nucleotides - adenine, guanine, cytosine, and thymine - make up the DNA that encodes the entire biology of life. They encode each cell that makes up our skin organ system. They encode proteins in that cell that allow for them to function, grow, check for external damage, and initiate processes that repair themselves when damage occurs. These four nucleotides control all the biological processes of our life.

Similarly, there are 4 basic spiritual building blocks I will refer to as "spiritualtides" that are critical for our spiritual growth. They are essential to monitor for spiritual damage and to initiate processes to begin repair when spiritual damage occurs. These spiritualtides are the first four principles of the Savior's gospel - faith, repentance, baptism (or partaking of the sacrament), and the reception of the Holy Ghost. Just like nucleotides contain the instructions to make proteins that carry out all cellular functions necessary for life, the four spiritual peptides can be connected together to form the basis of our entire spiritual experience that helps us as spiritual beings navigate through the mortal experiences of our life.

Elder Dale G. Renlund teaches that the process of faith, repentance, baptism, and the receiving of the Holy Ghost is not meant to be a one-time event. They are meant to be repeated just like a strand of DNA lays down each of the four peptides in repeating patterns. However, the four principles of the Gospel are more than just repetitive, they are also meant to be iterative - meaning that we change and improve with each cycle. A repeating DNA strand doesn't just go around and around but also winds upward in the shape of a climbing double helix. When we participate in the four principles of the Savior's gospel we follow a pattern of upward lifelong conversion that doesn't just send us spinning around and around in repetitive circles, but it is also meant to help us improve, change, become better, and spiral upward with each cycle. Elder Renlund teaches:

> "Each element in the doctrine of Christ builds on the preceding step—repentance builds on faith, baptism on repentance, and the gift of the Holy Ghost on baptism— and then the sequence recurs. Each cycle ends

progressively higher, so the subsequent cycle is higher and different. In this way the doctrine of Christ is iterative. Cycling iteratively through the elements of the doctrine of Christ enables us to endure to the end."[7]

Applying Christ's atonement in our lives is applying the building blocks of His gospel over and over. It is the process by which we allow the Savior to touch and heal our hearts and spirits from the damaging effects caused by our agency (sin) and helps us heal when we are damaged by the misused agency of others (forgiving and loving others). Through faith, we activate His power, and through repentance, we unlock and magnify His power. As we demonstrate our change of heart through participating in the sacrament ordinance, we are promised to have His Spirit if we covenant to be willing to take upon His name, keep His commandments, and always remember Him. The blessings of the Holy Ghost that he promises to send to us will comfort, bring all things to remembrance, warn, guide, and ultimately heal us.

By allowing His hands to be pierced and wounded, the Savior unlocked the power to allow His hands to heal our pierced and wounded hearts and minds. Although you may not have outer wounds like the leper who came to the Savior, we all have inner spiritual wounds. With His help and the help of the Holy Ghost, we can bring these spiritual wounds to him to be touched and healed.

Become the Touch of the Master's Hand

Many years ago, I worked with a man who was relearning this process of laying down the "spiritualtides" of faith, repentance, baptism, and receiving the Holy Ghost in his life. Due to previous choices, he was unable to fully participate in the iterative process of Christ's gospel for a period of time. However, he was able to be rebaptized and eagerly began fully participating in applying the four building blocks of Christ's gospel and was applying the atonement to qualify to have his priesthood blessings restored. I thought of the courage and strength this man showed despite feelings of inadequacy and disappointment that he had endured for many years as he worked to fully participate in the gospel. As the day approached for the potential restoration of his blessings, the spirit spoke strongly to my mind that I needed to ask him for a priesthood blessing so that I could be strengthened by him to face the challenges and trials happening at this time in my life. I told him I wanted to be the first person he blessed after his priesthood authority was restored. He later recalled how it meant so much to him that I asked him to lay his hands on my head to give me a blessing despite me being familiar with the long journey he had trod. I was able to be blessed with eyes to see this man as the Savior did - a child of God worthy of human touch - as he placed His hands upon my head and gave me a beautiful blessing. Not only was his priesthood restored that day but his feelings of value and self-worth were restored too.

In this experience, we can learn another lesson in the miracle of the leper. If we are to be disciples of Jesus Christ, we are called to support and heal rather than condemn those who are working to apply the atonement of Christ and the four principles of His gospel. Many of those engaged in this repentance process may feel neglected, brushed off, or abandoned by the very church members surrounding them. The man with leprosy was shunned, condemned, and ostracized from his society. He was convinced he had brought this outward-appearing disease upon himself because of an inward unworthiness. Because of this dogma, people around him were afraid to touch and love him. If we are to become as the Savior is, we must not be the shunner, the one who casts stones, or the priest who passes by the injured on the road of life. We must not be afraid to go to the rescue to provide healing hands as the Savior did. We must be willing to leave the comfort of the ninety-nine to go after the one. Elder

Uchtdorf shares a story of our call to become the Savior's hands.

> "A story is told that during the bombing of a city in World War II, a large statue of Jesus Christ was severely damaged. When the townspeople found the statue among the rubble, they mourned because it had been a beloved symbol of their faith and of God's presence in their lives.
>
> Experts were able to repair most of the statue, but its hands had been damaged so severely that they could not be restored. Some suggested that they hire a sculptor to make new hands, but others wanted to leave it as it was—a permanent reminder of the tragedy of war. Ultimately, the statue remained without hands. However, the people of the city added on the base of the statue of Jesus Christ a sign with these words: 'You are my hands.'"[8]

We can be the healing hands of the Savior as we reach out to comfort those around us. The Church is not a country club for saints, but a hospital for sinners. We all need the touch of the master's hand, and we all need to be the same healing hands that reach out and lift up those around us in need. We "give our hands" when we treat those who have sinned with kindness and respect, respond only with righteous judgment, and choose to see their divine potential. We become the Savior's hands when we walk the difficult path of repentance alongside them giving support and comfort instead of avoiding contact because of potentially awkward situations. If we see such individuals as the Savior sees them we will not gossip, shun, or avoid interactions with people working to access the healing power of the Savior. We will not run away *from* them, but instead, we'll run *to* them and support them in any way they need.

In like manner, we will do the same to those around us who are victims of the sins and misuse of agency by others. We must not view their challenges and misfortunes as a consequence of something they brought upon themselves, but instead extend hands of support and comfort devoid of judgment. Consider the powerful example of this by a young woman shared by Sister Michelle Craig at the 2020 October General Conference.

"[This] story was shared with me by my friend who was devastated when her husband of 20 years moved out. With her children splitting time between parents, the prospect of attending church alone seemed daunting. She recounts:

"In a church where the family is of paramount importance, sitting solo can be painful. That first Sunday I walked in praying no one would speak to me. I was barely holding it together, and tears were on the brink. I sat in my typical spot, hoping no one would notice how empty the bench seemed.

"A young woman in our ward turned and looked at me. I pretended to smile. She smiled back. I could see the concern in her face. I silently pleaded that she wouldn't come to talk to me—I had nothing positive to say and knew I would cry. I looked back down at my lap and avoided eye contact.

"During the next hour, I noticed her looking back at me occasionally. As soon as the meeting ended, she made a beeline for me. 'Hi, Rozlyn,' I whispered. She wrapped me in her arms and said, 'Sister Smith, I can tell today is a bad day for you. I'm so sorry. I love you.' As predicted, the tears came as she hugged me again. But as I walked away, I thought to myself, 'Maybe I can do this after all.'

"That sweet 16-year-old young woman, less than half my age, found me every Sunday for the rest of that year to give me a hug and ask, 'How are you?' It made such a difference in how I felt about coming to church. The truth is I started to rely on those hugs. Someone noticed me. Someone knew I was there. Someone cared."[9]

Personal Reflection:
1. In your recent interactions with others, have you noticed anyone who might be going through challenges?
2. Pray to have eyes to see to perceive the needs of others.
3. Pray for the strength and courage to act on the promptings you feel to become the Savior's Hands for those in need.

---

[1] Mark 1:33

[2] Matthew 4:24

[3] Leviticus 13, 14

[4] Leviticus 13:45

[5] Leviticus 14:4-7

[6] MacDonald, George. "The Miracles of Our Lord." (New York: George Routledge & Sons, 1870), pp. 88–89

[7] Dale G. Renlund. "Lifelong Conversion," BYU Speeches, Sept 4, 2021

[8] Deiter F. Uchtdorf. "You are My Hands," General Conference, April 2020

[9] Michelle Craig. "Eyes to See," General Conference, October 2020

Chapter 6

Jesus Heals the Paralytic

As Jesus traveled back to Capernaum, he performed the miracle of healing a servant of a Centurion soldier. This miracle is found in Matthew (8:5-13) and Luke (7:2-10). Although both contain similar themes, they also have distinct differences. In both accounts, a centurion has a servant who is ill. When Jesus indicates he will come to heal him, the centurion declares that he is unworthy of the Savior's presence in his house. He asks Jesus to speak the word of healing only. He references that as a centurion, based on his station and authority, he simply needs to speak only, and those under his command will fulfill his request. This person's faith marvels Jesus. He declares that none is found greater in all of Israel. The Savior's word then heals the servant.

However, the account details differ in several aspects. In Matthew's account, the Centurion came to Jesus to make his request, whereas in Luke's, he sent the elders of the Jews to Jesus to make his request for him. In case there was any doubt why such a man would be worthy to receive such a miracle, Luke emphasizes that the elders reminded Jesus of the centurion's generosity and love toward the Jews, evidenced by his previously building them a synagogue for worship. When Jesus indicated he would travel to the home to fulfill the request for healing, Matthew wrote that the Centurion told the Savior this was unnecessary and that he was unworthy to have him as a guest. However, in Luke's account, Jesus traveled toward the centurion's home with the elders of the Jews, and it wasn't until drawing close that he stopped the Savior. The centurion sent his friends out to meet the Savior and declare his unworthiness. In fact, in Luke 7:7, the Centurion, through his friends, states that he had never come unto the Lord in the first place because he considered himself unworthy of His presence.

Although we never learn what is troubling the servant in the account of Luke, based on Matthew's writing, we read that the servant is "grievously tormented" and sick by the palsy. Upon speaking the word of healing, the Centurion returned home in Matthew's account to find his servant "healed that self-same hour," whereas, in the record of Luke, the centurion's friends returned to the house to find him healed that same hour.

Account of Matthew:

> 5 And when Jesus was entered into Capernaum, there came unto him a centurion, beseeching him,
>
> 6 And saying, Lord, my servant lieth at home sick of the palsy, grievously tormented.
>
> 7 And Jesus saith unto him, I will come and heal him.
>
> 8 The centurion answered and said, Lord, I am not worthy that thou shouldest come under my roof: but speak the word only, and my servant shall be healed.
>
> 9 For I am a man under authority, having soldiers under me: and I say to this man, Go, and he goeth; and to another, Come, and he cometh; and to my servant, Do this, and he doeth it.
>
> 10 When Jesus heard it, he marvelled, and said to them that followed, Verily I say unto you, I have not found so great faith, no, not in Israel.
>
> 11 And I say unto you, That many shall come from the east and west, and shall sit down with Abraham, and Isaac, and Jacob, in the kingdom of heaven.
>
> 12 But the children of the kingdom shall be cast out into outer darkness: there shall be weeping and gnashing of teeth.
>
> 13 And Jesus said unto the centurion, Go thy way; and as thou hast believed, so be it done unto thee. And his servant was healed in the selfsame hour.

Account of Luke:

2 And a certain centurion's servant, who was dear unto him, was sick, and ready to die.

3 And when he heard of Jesus, he sent unto him the elders of the Jews, beseeching him that he would come and heal his servant.

4 And when they came to Jesus, they besought him instantly, saying, That he was worthy for whom he should do this:

5 For he loveth our nation, and he hath built us a synagogue.

6 Then Jesus went with them. And when he was now not far from the house, the centurion sent friends to him, saying unto him, Lord, trouble not thyself: for I am not worthy that thou shouldest enter under my roof:

7 Wherefore neither thought I myself worthy to come unto thee: but say in a word, and my servant shall be healed.

8 For I also am a man set under authority, having under me soldiers, and I say unto one, Go, and he goeth; and to another, Come, and he cometh; and to my servant, Do this, and he doeth it.

9 When Jesus heard these things, he marvelled at him, and turned him about, and said unto the people that followed him, I say unto you, I have not found so great faith, no, not in Israel.

10 And they that were sent, returning to the house, found the servant whole that had been sick.

Later, in Matthew chapter 8, another paralyzed man is brought to the Savior on a bed. The scribes thought it was blasphemy for Jesus to pronounce forgiveness for sins before the miracle of healing. Jesus taught that just as He could do the spiritually impossible (forgive sins), He also had the power to do the physically impossible (heal paralysis). The power to do so is the same. He told the man to rise and carry his bed back to his house. Everyone marveled at the Savior's power.

> 2 And, behold, they brought to him a man sick of the palsy, lying on a bed: and Jesus seeing their faith said unto the sick of the palsy; Son, be of good cheer; thy sins be forgiven thee.
> 3 And, behold, certain of the scribes said within themselves, This man blasphemeth.
> 4 And Jesus knowing their thoughts said, Wherefore think ye evil in your hearts?
> 5 For whether is easier, to say, Thy sins be forgiven thee; or to say, Arise, and walk?
> 6 But that ye may know that the Son of man hath power on earth to forgive sins, (then saith he to the sick of the palsy,) Arise, take up thy bed, and go unto thine house.
> 7 And he arose, and departed to his house.
> 8 But when the multitudes saw it, they marvelled, and glorified God, which had given such power unto men.

On a third occasion, the Savior also healed a man with a condition that prevented him from walking. This man waited, along with many other people suffering from other medical conditions, near the side of the Pool of Bethesda. At a certain time, when the water was stirred, the pool was believed to have healing powers. However, this man had waited thirty-eight years to be healed because his condition prevented him from getting into the water when it was stirred. Jesus told him to rise, take his bed, walk, and immediately healed the man. In John 5, we read:

> 2 Now there is at Jerusalem by the sheep market a pool, which is called in the Hebrew tongue Bethesda, having five porches.

3 In these lay a great multitude of impotent folk, of blind, halt, withered, waiting for the moving of the water.

4 For an angel went down at a certain season into the pool, and troubled the water: whosoever then first after the troubling of the water stepped in was made whole of whatsoever disease he had.

5 And a certain man was there, which had an infirmity thirty and eight years.

6 When Jesus saw him lie, and knew that he had been now a long time in that case, he saith unto him, Wilt thou be made whole?

7 The impotent man answered him, Sir, I have no man, when the water is troubled, to put me into the pool: but while I am coming, another steppeth down before me.

8 Jesus saith unto him, Rise, take up thy bed, and walk.

9 And immediately the man was made whole, and took up his bed, and walked: and on the same day was the sabbath.

The Miracle of the Neuromuscular System

The body's movement requires constant communication via the neuromuscular system between the brain and the muscles. Movement is a miracle. The process of lifting one's arm seems relatively straightforward. However, it is a complex coordination of electrical and chemical signals occurring in multiple brain locations, spinal cord, and muscle areas. Although entire textbooks have been written, devoting multiple chapters to each step, a summary for the reader will hopefully cultivate an appreciation for the everyday miracle of even simple movements.

Each nerve sends signals along its pathway by opening channels in the nerve's cell membrane, allowing sodium ions to flow into the nerve cell. Like dominoes that propagate down a row as they fall, the opening of a sodium channel activates adjacent sodium channels and continues the signal down the length of the nerve. They are called electrical impulses because a nerve at rest has a large concentration of positively charged sodium ions on the outside of the cell membrane and a greater concentration of negatively charged chloride ions on the inside of the nerve. This voltage difference creates a charge across the cell membrane, much like the difference between a battery's positive and negative ends. When sodium channels at the beginning of a nerve open, sodium ions flow into the cell, negatively charged chloride ions flow out of the cell, and the electrical signal propagates down the nerve.

A familiar example of this electrical phenomenon is "the wave" at a sporting event. The initial sodium channel opening is similar to when someone lifts their arms to start the wave. If a critical mass of people raise their arms at the initial location, the wave continues around the stadium. This process continues until the signal moves from one end of the stadium to the other, or in other words, the beginning of a nerve to the end of the nerve. Sometimes, a few people try to start the wave at first, but it dies out quickly. However, if a critical mass can initiate and propagate "the wave," then the momentum carries the wave around the stadium. In like manner, nerves receive multiple electrochemical inputs. Some may be insufficient to initiate the propagation of nerve transmission down the axon of the nerve. However, when sufficient input is received at the beginning of the nerve, similar to when an adequate number of people lift their arms to start the wave, the wave continues uninterrupted down the nerve. This process is known as depolarization; at a resting state, the nerve is polarized with positive charges on the outside and negative charges on the inside. When the nerve is activated, it depolarizes. When depolarization occurs beyond a certain threshold, then an action potential occurs. An action potential is an all-or-nothing event where nerve activation can no longer be restrained, and the nerve signal propagates the length of the nerve.

At the end of each nerve, chemicals called neurotransmitters are stored in packages called vesicles. When the electrical wave gets to the end of the nerve, vesicles fuse to the end membrane of the nerve and release the neurotransmitters into the space between the end of one nerve and the beginning of another. Nerves are interconnected with many other nerves called interneurons. Consequently, each nerve can receive neurotransmitters from many different sources. The neurotransmitters can be excitatory (propagating the signal), inhibitory (attempting to terminate the signal), or modulatory (modifying the degree of excitation or inhibition). Although over 100 neurotransmitters are known, the most common excitatory neurotransmitter is glutamate, the most common inhibitory transmitter is GABA, and the most common modulatory transmitter is dopamine. Each nerve receives the modulatory, excitatory, and inhibitory chemicals continuously. If the sum of the signals exceeds the threshold at any time, then an action potential occurs, propagating the all-or-nothing impulse to the end of the nerve.

Returning to the stadium wave analogy, this can appear to be a relatively slow process as one waits for the wave to come around for one's turn to lift one's hands. The nerve conduction process can be accelerated when nerve support cells called Schwann cells produce myelin that insulates the nerves. Myelin is a fatty substance that protects the nerves to prevent electrical signal loss. Gaps of myelin occur at regular intervals and are called Nodes of Ranvier. The nerve electrical signals play a game of leapfrog, jumping from node to node instead of traveling the entire distance - one sodium channel at a time - along the nerve. In other words, instead of requiring the wave at the stadium to travel from person to person, with the existence of the Nodes of Ranvier, as soon as one person lifts their arms in a section of seats, the following section lifts their arms. This increase in nerve conduction speed is significant; jumping from node to node in a process called saltatory conduction moves the electrical impulse at a rate of 150 meters a second compared to the speed of conduction for unmyelinated nerves, which, depending on the type of the nerve, can be as slow as 0.5 to 10 meters per second.

With a basic understanding of nerves and their function, let's review the pathway this signal must take from thought to arm movement. First, neurons in the brain's frontal cortex, the executive function or decision-maker part of your brain, decide to lift your left arm. Communication from the frontal cortex sends the signal via nerves to the area of the brain containing the motor nerves to initiate the process in the right brain. The motor neurons then send the electrical signal down through a deep brain structure known as the internal capsule of the thalamus. The nerve signals travel from the thalamus down through the midbrain and cross over from the right side of the corticospinal tract to the left side to communicate with another set of neurons originating at the upper part of the spinal cord. The signal continues down the spinal cord until the central nervous system connects with the peripheral nervous system.

The impulse then travels along peripheral nerves that contact a muscle at the neuromuscular junction (NMJ). At this location, the electrical signal triggers the opening of calcium channels that cause acetylcholine vesicles to fuse to the end of the nerve cell and release the acetylcholine into the NMJ. When acetylcholine binds to the motor end plate receptors of the muscle, it causes a conformational change like a key in a lock. The acetylcholine key opens the flow of sodium ions again into the muscle cell, causing the signal to travel through the muscle.

This signal to contract travels through channels called T-tubules deep into each muscle fiber's inner core called the sarcoplasmic reticulum. Once again, this signal triggers the opening of calcium channels that allow calcium to diffuse into each muscle fiber cell. The calcium interacts with the sarcomere, the workhorse of the muscle cell. When the calcium binds to a protein called troponin, it causes a conformational change and pulls on the protein tropomyosin to shorten the sarcomere. Like the hand-over-hand pulling of a rope, this shortening continues, and the muscle shortens or contracts as long as there is sufficient calcium to trigger a contraction and cellular energy in the form of ATP to prime the troponin/tropomyosin complex to be ready for contraction. When this happens in the bicep muscle, the muscle shortens, while relaxation (lengthening) occurs in the tricep muscle, and the left forearm raises.

Physical Paralysis

The human body has around 7 trillion nerves, and the total length of the nerves spans about 37 miles. To take a single step, approximately 200 muscle contractions and 300-400 nerve impulses per nerve per second are required to perform this task. With all that could go wrong along the neuromuscular pathway, it is a miracle it works so often and so accurately.

Many diseases affecting normal neuromuscular function can occur in any part along the pathway. Stroke (death of brain cells due to decreased blood flow and oxygen delivery to areas of the brain), cerebral palsy (brain damage of motor areas during development), multiple sclerosis (nerve demyelination of central nervous system), Parkinson's disease (damage of nerve cells that produce dopamine that helps facilitate smooth and coordinated movements), and epilepsy (continued over-excited areas of the brain that lead to seizures) are just a few common examples of disease that occur in the brain and can affect movement. Trauma (spinal cord tearing, severing, or swelling that leads to decreased oxygen delivery), Guillain-barre (immune system attack of the nerve body leading to temporary or permanent loss of nerve function), ALS (progressive death of motor nerves and scarring of the spinal cord, loss of muscle function, and permanent atrophy of muscles because they receive no input), and transverse myelitis (inflammation of the spinal cord leading to loss of myelin) are a few of the more common causes of paralysis or movement disorders at the level of the spinal cord.

As for peripheral nerves, nerve entrapment, trauma, autoimmune diseases, chronic inflammation from diabetes, smoking, and vitamin deficiencies can lead to movement disorders originating at the peripheral nerves. Finally, at the muscular level, muscular dystrophy (genetic mutations that disrupt muscle integrity leading to loss of strength and function), Myasthenia Gravis and Lambert Eaton (antibodies against receptors at the neuromuscular junction) are just a few examples. This brief list is by no means complete. However, the reader should appreciate that given all that can go wrong, it is a miracle how often things go right!

Spiritual Paralysis

While palsy is a form of physical paralysis, perhaps more detrimental to our movement on the covenant path of the gospel of Jesus Christ is spiritual paralysis. Just as the physical movement pathways are complex, with many diseases that disrupt the movement pathway, many things may interrupt our spiritual progression, leaving us in spiritual paralysis.

Avoiding spiritual paralysis is so paramount in our time that many messages and invitations extended by President Nelson since becoming the prophet are aimed at helping us continually move forward on the covenant path. His first message as prophet was to encourage members to keep moving on the covenant path. He pleaded,

> "Keep on the covenant path. Your commitment to follow the Savior by making covenants with Him and then keeping those covenants will open the door to

every spiritual blessing and privilege available to men, women and children everywhere."[1]

In his first general conference address as the prophet in April 2018, he urged us to seek, qualify for, and act on personal revelation. He warned that "in the coming days, it will not be possible to survive spiritually without the guiding, directing, comforting, and constant influence of the Holy Ghost."[2]

One of the ways to experience the influence of the Holy Ghost in our life is through daily repentance, the topic he addressed the following year in 2019. The Bible Dictionary teaches that repentance is the process by which we move our hearts and will to God and move away from sin and disobedience that we are naturally inclined to. President Nelson addressed the topic of repentance the following year in 2019. He said, "I plead with you to repent. Experience the strengthening power of daily repentance — of doing and being a little better each day."[3] In 2020, he invited us to "Hear Him" so that we can be guided by the Savior to "know what to do in any circumstance."[4] And in 2021, he invited us to take extraordinary and unprecedented measures to strengthen our spiritual foundation.[5] All of these invitations are made to assist us in overcoming spiritual paralysis and keep us moving on the covenant path.

But President Nelson doesn't just want us to keep moving. He has asked us to increase our ability to move forward spiritually by asking us, "What can ignite positive spiritual momentum?"[6] The equation for momentum is $P = M \times V$. Momentum (P) is equal to mass (M) multiplied by velocity (V). Velocity has both speed and direction. We can have a speed of movement in our "busy" lives. However, without an added spiritual vector of direction that leads us to put off the natural man and become a saint through the atonement of Christ, our speed doesn't meaningfully contribute to our spiritual velocity. Therefore, it fails to help us have spiritual momentum. Our spiritual mass increases when the total of our natural man tendencies decrease, and instead, we change and act more like saints as King Benjamin taught. Through daily repentance, our spiritual mass increases. And, our momentum increases regardless of how small our velocity may still be. Even though physical and emotional challenges may restrict our velocity, increasing spiritual mass through daily repentance increases our momentum.

As we increase our spiritual momentum, our opportunity to help strengthen others on the covenant path also increases. Newton's second law states that when force is applied to an object at rest, it can cause it to accelerate in the direction and magnitude of the force applied to it. In gospel terms, as we "bump into others" through life, we can transfer spiritual momentum to those around us and bring them to a higher level of spiritual momentum. Living our lives with a focus on the two great commandments - loving God and loving our neighbor - we will be inclined to let our light shine so that others can see our good works and glorify Heavenly Father. We will naturally share our testimonies of the Savior Jesus Christ and his gospel with others we meet. We will courageously extend effective invitations for others to join the journey on the covenant path. In other words, with increased spiritual momentum, we will love, share, and invite others to improve their spiritual momentum. As we concurrently focus and act on things that increase our spiritual momentum it will magnify our ability to encourage and motivate others to follow.

Reflection:
1. What is one thing that prevents me from increasing my spiritual momentum that I can stop doing?
2. What is one thing that I can start doing to increase my spiritual mass or spiritual velocity and, therefore increase my spiritual momentum on the covenant path?
3. How can I encourage and assist others to increase their spiritual momentum on the covenant path?

[1] Lloyd, Scott. "President Russell N. Nelson Named 17th President of the Church," January 16, 2018. Newsroom. (https://www.churchofjesuschrist.org/church/news/president-russell-m-nelson-named-17th-president-of-the-church?lang=eng)

[2] Russell M. Nelson. "Revelations for the Church, Revelation for Our Lives." General Conference, April 2018

[3] Russell M. Nelson. "We Can Do Better and Be Better," General Conference, April 2019

[4] Russell M. Nelson. "Hear Him," General Conference, April 2020

[5] Russell M. Nelson. "The Temple and Your Spiritual Foundation," General Conference, October 2021)

[6] Russell M. Nelson. "The Power of Spiritual Momentum," General Conference, April 2022

Chapter 7

Jesus Raises the Dead

The day after the Savior healed the centurion's servant, he traveled to a city called Nain. There, he encountered a crowd of people following a dead man being carried to his place of burial. He was the young son of a widow known only as the "widow of Nain." Jesus was filled with compassion upon seeing her. He comforted the widow, touched the bier (frame carrying the corpse), and commanded the young man to arise. The young man sat up, spoke, and went to his mother. This miracle is written only in the gospel of Luke, chapter 7.

> 11 ¶ And it came to pass the day after, that he went into a city called Nain; and many of his disciples went with him, and much people.
> 12 Now when he came nigh to the gate of the city, behold, there was a dead man carried out, the only son of his mother, and she was a widow: and much people of the city was with her.
> 13 And when the Lord saw her, he had compassion on her, and said unto her, Weep not.
> 14 And he came and touched the bier: and they that bare him stood still. And he said, Young man, I say unto thee, Arise.
> 15 And he that was dead sat up, and began to speak. And he delivered him to his mother.
> 16 And there came a fear on all: and they glorified God, saying, That a great prophet is risen up among us; and, That God hath visited his people.
> 17 And this rumour of him went forth throughout all Judæa, and throughout all the region round about.

Keith Wilson, a professor of ancient scripture at Brigham Young University and former teacher at the BYU Jerusalem

Center, describes the unique timing critical to appreciating the deep compassion the Savior had on this woman and the ability of the Savior to intervene in our lives at precisely the right moment. He points out that the Savior and His disciples went into the city of Nain "the day after" He healed the centurion's servant in Capernaum. Nain is a small village city approximately 30 miles southwest of Capernaum and accessible at the time only by a single dirt road. Furthermore, Capernaum is situated 600 feet below sea level, while Nain is located 700 feet above sea level. In short, the journey is long and uphill. Professor Wilson points out that at the time of Jesus, travel like this would usually take 1-2 days. Recently, with his BYU students traveling on paved roads, the trip took approximately 10 hours.[1] This meant that for Jesus to meet the procession at precisely the necessary time before the widow of Nain son's burial, he would have had to either travel through the night or intentionally rise extra early to begin the journey to Nain.

On three additional occasions, Jesus performed the miracle of raising life from the dead. In Matthew chapter 9, a ruler named Jarius came to Jesus and asked Him to bring his daughter back from the dead. When He eventually made it to the house after healing the woman with an issue of blood, Jesus was mocked by those surrounding Jarius' daughter when Jesus declared that she was sleeping and not dead. He came and took the young woman by the hand and she arose.

> 18 While he spake these things unto them, behold, there came a certain ruler, and worshipped him, saying, My daughter is even now dead: but come and lay thy hand upon her, and she shall live.
> 19 And Jesus arose, and followed him, and so did his disciples.
> 23 And when Jesus came into the ruler's house, and saw the minstrels and the people making a noise,

> 24 He said unto them, Give place: for the maid is not dead, but sleepeth. And they laughed him to scorn.
> 25 But when the people were put forth, he went in, and took her by the hand, and the maid arose.
> 26 And the fame hereof went abroad into all that land.

As if there were still any doubts as to whether Jesus in life had power over death, He sought to lay that question to rest with the account of raising Lazarus from the dead. In John chapter 11, Mary and Martha, the sisters of Lazarus, informed Jesus of his sickness. Instead of traveling immediately, Jesus tarried for two days to tell them that Lazarus would not die, but that he was sick so that "the glory of God, that the Son of God might be glorified thereby."[2] A humorous exchange between Christ's disciples then occurred. The disciples told Jesus that if Lazarus was just sleeping, they shouldn't bother him and let him sleep. Jesus needed to be a little more direct and told his disciples plainly, "Lazarus is dead."[3]

By the time Jesus arrived, Lazarus had been in the tomb for four days. His sisters, Mary and Martha, were so devastated that many of the Jews had come to comfort them. Even though Martha expresses faith in an eventual resurrection, she tells Jesus if he had come, Lazarus wouldn't have died. Jesus takes this opportunity to testify that he is the reason for the resurrection and has power over death then and now. Jesus also allows her to declare her testimony. Even though Jesus knew He would raise Lazarus from the dead, Jesus had such deep compassion for Mary and the Jews with her who were weeping over Lazarus' death that Jesus, too, wept with them.[4]

Jesus' love for Martha seems to soften her heart. With renewed faith, she testified that whatever Jesus asked of God, God would grant unto him. [5] Because of this expression of faith, the manner of raising Lazarus from the dead was different from other miracles. Instead of performing the miracle, Jesus first prayed to God to give thanks for always listening to him before commanding Lazarus to come forth.[6] Lazarus, still bound by the burial clothes, came out of the grave to the astonishment of all present and caused many to believe in Jesus.

> 3 Therefore his sisters sent unto him, saying, Lord, behold, he whom thou lovest is sick.
> 4 When Jesus heard that, he said, This sickness is not unto death, but for the glory of God, that the Son of God might be glorified thereby.
> 5 Now Jesus loved Martha, and her sister, and Lazarus.
> 6 When he had heard therefore that he was sick, he bode two days still in the same place where he was.
> 7 Then after that saith he to his disciples, Let us go into Judæa again.
> 8 His disciples say unto him, Master, the Jews of late sought to stone thee; and goest thou thither again?
> 9 Jesus answered, Are there not twelve hours in the day? If any man walk in the day, he stumbleth not, because he seeth the light of this world.
> 10 But if a man walk in the night, he stumbleth, because there is no light in him.
> 11 These things said he: and after that he saith unto them, Our friend Lazarus sleepeth; but I go, that I may awake him out of sleep.
> 12 Then said his disciples, Lord, if he sleep, he shall do well.
> 13 Howbeit Jesus spake of his death: but they thought that he had spoken of taking of rest in sleep.
> 14 Then said Jesus unto them plainly, Lazarus is dead.
> 15 And I am glad for your sakes that I was not there, to the intent ye may believe; nevertheless let us go unto him.
> 16 Then said Thomas, which is called Didymus, unto his fellow disciples, Let us also go, that we may die with him.

17 Then when Jesus came, he found that he had lain in the grave four days already.

18 Now Bethany was nigh unto Jerusalem, about fifteen furlongs off:

19 And many of the Jews came to Martha and Mary, to comfort them concerning their brother.

20 Then Martha, as soon as she heard that Jesus was coming, went and met him: but Mary sat still in the house.

21 Then said Martha unto Jesus, Lord, if thou hadst been here, my brother had not died.

22 But I know, that even now, whatsoever thou wilt ask of God, God will give it thee.

23 Jesus saith unto her, Thy brother shall rise again.

24 Martha saith unto him, I know that he shall rise again in the resurrection at the last day.

25 Jesus said unto her, I am the resurrection, and the life: he that believeth in me, though he were dead, yet shall he live:

26 And whosoever liveth and believeth in me shall never die. Believest thou this?

27 She saith unto him, Yea, Lord: I believe that thou art the Christ, the Son of God, which should come into the world.

28 And when she had so said, she went her way, and called Mary her sister secretly, saying, The Master is come, and calleth for thee.

29 As soon as she heard that, she arose quickly, and came unto him.

30 Now Jesus was not yet come into the town, but was in that place where Martha met him.

31 The Jews then which were with her in the house, and comforted her, when they saw Mary, that she rose up hastily and went out, followed her, saying, She goeth unto the grave to weep there.

32 Then when Mary was come where Jesus was, and saw him, she fell down at his feet, saying unto him, Lord, if thou hadst been here, my brother had not died.

33 When Jesus therefore saw her weeping, and the Jews also weeping which came with her, he groaned in the spirit, and was troubled,

34 And said, Where have ye laid him? They said unto him, Lord, come and see.

35 Jesus wept.

36 Then said the Jews, Behold how he loved him!

37 And some of them said, Could not this man, which opened the eyes of the blind, have caused that even this man should not have died?

38 Jesus therefore again groaning in himself cometh to the grave. It was a cave, and a stone lay upon it.

39 Jesus said, Take ye away the stone. Martha, the sister of him that was dead, saith unto him, Lord, by this time he stinketh: for he hath been dead four days.

40 Jesus saith unto her, Said I not unto thee, that, if thou wouldest believe, thou shouldest see the glory of God?

41 Then they took away the stone from the place where the dead was laid. And Jesus lifted up his eyes, and said, Father, I thank thee that thou hast heard me.

42 And I knew that thou hearest me always: but because of the people which stand by I said it, that they may believe that thou hast sent me.

43 And when he thus had spoken, he cried with a loud voice, Lazarus, come forth.

44 And he that was dead came forth, bound hand and foot with graveclothes: and his face was bound about with a napkin. Jesus saith unto them, Loose him, and let him go.

45 Then many of the Jews which came to Mary, and had seen the things which Jesus did, believed on him.

46 But some of them went their ways to the Pharisees, and told them what things Jesus had done.

Finally, the fourth person Jesus raised from the dead was himself. In Luke, chapter 24, we read the account of three women - Mary Magdalene, Joanna, and Mary, the mother of James - who came to the tomb to bring prepared spices to dress the body of Jesus. However, upon arrival, they found that the tomb was empty. In their confusion, two angels appeared and taught them that "He is not here, but he is risen."[7] Jesus not only had the power to bring back the son of the widow of Nain, the daughter of Jarius, and Lazarus. He also had the power to bring *His* body back from the dead.

1 Now upon the first day of the week, very early in the morning, they came unto the sepulchre, bringing the spices which they had prepared, and certain others with them.
2 And they found the stone rolled away from the sepulchre.
3 And they entered in, and found not the body of the Lord Jesus.
4 And it came to pass, as they were much perplexed thereabout, behold, two men stood by them in shining garments:
5 And as they were afraid, and bowed down their faces to the earth, they said unto them, Why seek ye the living among the dead?
6 He is not here, but is risen: remember how he spake unto you when he was yet in Galilee,
7 Saying, The Son of man must be delivered into the hands of sinful men, and be crucified, and the third day rise again.
8 And they remembered his words,
9 And returned from the sepulchre, and told all these things unto the eleven, and to all the rest.

The Miracle of Life and Death

As a physician anesthesiologist, I have had the unique privilege of being present at the time that individuals are born into or pass out of this life. What starts as the fusion of one sperm with an egg containing 23 chromosomes, this newly formed zygote rapidly divides and doubles in cell number over the next several days. Within two weeks of fertilization, cells differentiate into specific structures and functions. Primitive digestive, neurological, and cardiovascular tracts connected to a beating heart are formed. As early as three weeks, red blood cells begin to circulate. In only 8-10 weeks almost all organs are completely formed. At 12 weeks, the baby has filled the entire uterus, and at week 16, the gender of the baby can be identified. Sometime shortly after and by 20 weeks, the mother can begin to sense fetal movement. By week 24, the baby can survive entirely outside of the mother's womb if born prematurely.

Upon entering the world, the umbilical cord connecting the child to the mother's placenta, from which the baby has received all nutrients and oxygen for the last nine months, is clamped. This clamping dramatically increases resistance to blood flow out of the fetal heart, which facilitates the closure of cardiac shunts in the fetal heart. These shunts exist because blood flow doesn't need to become oxygenated by the baby's lungs while in utero. With the umbilical cord clamping, the blood now enters the lungs instead of flowing to the placenta. As the baby takes its first breath, the lower relative pressure in the chest cavity from the contraction of the diaphragm muscle further promotes blood flow into the lungs. Newborn blood begins to circulate and oxygenate independently of material support. The newborn baby quickly transforms into the color of life. Witnessing the birth of a child and the first breath of life is truly awe-inspiring!

At some point, however, we return to our God who has given us life. Death is medically defined as 1) the irreversible cessation of respiratory or cardiac function or 2) the irreversible cessation of all functions of the brain and brainstem. At death, the body begins to undergo seemingly irreversible processes. Within minutes of the cessation of blood circulation, the body starts to appear pale as gravity begins to drain blood out of the smaller capillary vessels on the skin's surface. The skin starts to sag, the tone of all muscles begins to relax, and the relaxation of muscles may cause loss of bowel or bladder contents. The core temperature of the body drops from its average temperature of 37 degrees Celsius at a rate of approximately 1.5 degrees per hour until room temperature. The approximate time of death can, therefore, be estimated by body temperature when death is unwitnessed.

Within several hours, the pooling of blood due to gravity causes a purple discoloration that resembles a bruise on the underside of the body. Chemical changes occur within the muscles, transforming them from a relaxed to a stiffened state known as rigor mortis. This stiffening of muscles progresses stepwise, beginning in the face, then the torso, and eventually distally to the muscles of the arms, legs, fingers, and toes. This process continues for several hours until about 8-12 hours when the limbs become difficult to move, and the joints appear frozen in a contracted state.

As time continues, however, the rigor mortis process reverses in the same manner it began, and the body begins to relax progressively in a process known as secondary flaccidity. This progressive muscle relaxation occurs over the next few days while the skin retracts, giving the illusion of hair or nail growth.

Although we don't know the exact time of death of the widow of Nain's only son, likely, the funeral procession occurred no more than a day after death. Unlike the Egyptians, the Israelites did not preserve a deceased body with an embalming process. Given the hot climate, a prompt burial was imperative according to Jewish custom. The body was likely wrapped in cloth, as was the case with Lazarus, instead of an expensive coffin, and carried out on a bier (a stretcher for carrying deceased bodies) to the place of burial. Although paying final respects to deceased persons was considered important, delaying a burial longer than three days to allow people to travel to do so was often prohibited.

Understanding what happens to the body when one starts to die underscores the miracle of Jesus and his ability to bring it back to life. The cellular processes that cause the muscles to go through rigor mortis and secondary flaccidity need to be reversed. The blood that pooled due to gravity and likely started to clot because of lack of circulation would need to reliquify, circulate, and once again effectively carry oxygen on hemoglobin to all of the body's cells. As the creator of all things from the beginning, Jesus perfectly understands all the laws of nature. With this perfect knowledge, He would know how to restart our body's cellular processes and restore life.

Ministering to the One

Although the widow of Nain's son is the first documented miracle of Jesus' power over life, what is striking is that it does not appear to be the primary focus of Luke's attention. In verse 13, Luke does not state "when the Lord saw the dead body," "when the Lord saw the dead young man," or "when the Lord saw the corpse." Instead, Luke focuses on the widow of Nain and writes, "and when the Lord saw **her.**" It was the compassion that the Savior had for the weeping mother mourning over the loss of her only son that captured Luke's attention.

The Savior knew the plight of the widow of Nain. She had lost her husband, and now, having lost her only son, she would become destitute in society. He knew that she would likely neither have access to inheritance nor have the opportunity to provide for herself financially due to the disparities of women at the time. She was worse off than Naomi, who had the fortunate help of her daughter-in-law Ruth. If lucky, perhaps she could find a field of Boaz from which she may glean left behind crops for food, but in a village with as few as 34 homes, and even in modern times only has approximately 1500 inhabitants, finding someone willing like Boaz would be unlikely.

Further complicating her plight was the Old Testament belief that the premature death of a husband was a sign of sin and that the surviving widow was receiving the judgments and punishment of God. After burying her only hope, she likely was facing financial impossibilities, societal loneliness, and spiritual depression.

However, she may have captured the attention of the Savior for another reason. Perhaps this was an opportunity for Jesus to perform and act in similitude with his divine character and role as the Savior of the world. Luke states that the deceased son is the "only son" of his mother. In the original Greek, the word used to describe the only son is the word "monogenes." This same word is used to describe God's relationship to Jesus and translates from Greek as the "only begotten son." The widow's only begotten son being brought back from the dead would not only heal her broken heart but would also allow her to live. Similarly, Jesus, as the Father's only begotten son, was given the power to rise again after his death with "healing in his wings"[8] to give life to all the world. As stated so eloquently in John 3:16,

> "For God so loved the world, that he gave his only begotten Son, that whosoever believeth in him should not perish, but have everlasting life"

Jesus Christ went great lengths to bring healing to the widow of Nain in the very hour that she needed. In like manner, because of God's great love for each of us, he has sent

Jesus Christ to the world to offer this same power and healing.

Jesus particularly extends this love and compassion for women in the Bible overcome by grief due to the passing of loved ones. Even though Christ knew in a few moments he would be calling Lazarus from the grave, He paused to "mourn with those who mourn, and comfort those who stand in need of being comforted."[9] He wept with Mary and the Jews. He chose to experience the grief over the current loss of their friend Lazarus *WITH* them. By experiencing this emotion, they could more fully experience the joy of having Lazarus brought back from the dead.

Just as the Savior went to great lengths to bring peace, comfort, and life to the widow of Nain, Jesus can do the same for you and me. Adversity, discouragement, trials, temptation, and disappointment are an inevitable part of life. However, we need not suffer alone. As we sing in the hymn, "I Need thee Every Hour," if we rely on the Savior's grace, "in joy or pain," He can "come quickly and abide" so that life is not vain. It is important to note that the Savior "[went] forth, suffering pains and afflictions and temptations of *EVERY* kind."[10] He did this so that he might know exactly how we feel so that he would know precisely how to help us.

The first line in the next verse has always been particularly tender to me. "Now the Spirit knoweth all things, nevertheless the Son God suffereth according to the flesh."[11] The Savior wasn't satisfied just with cognitive learning of what we are going through in our individual lives. He wasn't satisfied with only being informed by the Spirit on what he should do to help us when we face pain, hopelessness, or discouragement. Jesus wanted experiential knowledge. He wanted to experience what we are experiencing. What does Jesus do with this knowledge? Adam Miller explains what this means to him.

> "Christ not only relieves my suffering, he also redeems my suffering. He relieves my suffering by sharing the

yoke of that suffering with me, by vicariously suffering whatever I may be suffering, be it pain or sickness or sin or death. In Christ, I'm never alone. In Christ, I'm never abandoned."[12]

Don't you feel more inclined to turn to the Savior, knowing that He truly knows how you feel and how to help you? Not only is the Savior's power a redemptive power (i.e. overcoming the effects of death and sin) by bringing the widow of Nain's son from the dead, it is an enabling power. Through Christ's grace, we can receive the strength to survive and thrive in life's ups and downs.

Elder Bednar taught that this enabling power gave Nephi strength to break the bands of the cords that his brothers used to tie him up while on the ship traveling toward the promised land.[13] The Lord didn't simply remove them. Furthermore, he didn't take away the afflictions of the people of Alma that were placed upon them by the priests of Amulon. Instead, the Lord strengthened them and lightened their burdens. In fact, they could "bear up their burdens with ease...cheerfully."[14] When Alma and Amulek were imprisoned and beaten after watching many of the saints suffer death, they received strength "even unto deliverance."[15] Likewise, the Savior can come to you and me in our moment of need, intervene, and give us the strength needed to overcome the trials we face. I echo Professor Wilson's sentiment regarding the miracle of the widow of Nain.

> "Of all Jesus's miracles during His time on earth, for me, few are as tender and compassionate as His ministering to the widow of Nain. It reminds us that we matter to Him and that He will never forget us. We cannot forget that."[16]

Reflection:
1. How has the Savior helped me in my time of need?

2. What can I do to rely on the mercy and merits of the Savior more fully?
3. How can I follow the example of Jesus to help others in their moment of need?

---

[1] Wilson, Keith. "In Times of Discouragement, Remember the Widow of Nain," Liahona, April 2019

[2] John 11:4

[3] John 11:14

[4] John 11:33-35

[5] John 11:22

[6] John 11:41-42

[7] Luke 24:6

[8] 2 Nephi 25:13, 3 Nephi 25:2

[9] Romans 12:15 and Mosiah 18:9

[10] Alma 7:12 (emphasis added)

[11] Alma 7:12

[12] Miller, Adam. Original Grace. Deseret Book, page 62

[13] David Bednar. "In the Strength of the Lord," BYU Speech, October 23, 2001

[14] Mosiah 24:15

[15] Alma 14:26

[16] [16] Wilson, Keith. "In Times of Discouragement, Remember the Widow of Nain," Liahona, April 2019

Chapter 8

Jesus Stills the Storm

The Savior commanded his disciples to enter boats and travel to Gergesenes on the western side of the Sea of Galilee to avoid the crowds of gathering people. A violent storm covered the ships with waves, and the disciples felt they would soon perish. By His word, the Savior calmed the winds and the waves, much to the marvel of His disciples. The account of Jesus bringing peace to a storm is in all four gospels and appears to have occurred on two separate occasions.

One occasion, detailed in the books of Matthew, Mark, and Luke, shares an account of the disciples in a storm at sea while the Savior slept. In each record, Jesus and his disciples attempt to leave many people by crossing the Sea of Galilee. In Matthew's account, the disciples follow Jesus entering the boat. However, in Mark and Luke's records, the disciples took Jesus into the boat and departed with other ships. The accounts agree upon the magnitude of the threatening storm - "the ship was covered with waves" (Matthew), that the waves" beat into the ship, so that it was now full" (Mark), or "they were filled with water and were in jeopardy" (Luke). In all accounts, the Savior was asleep during the storm, though Mark specifies he was in the back portion of the boat near the rudder. Furthermore, all agree they thought they would perish. Although he rebuked the winds and the waves, Mark adds the detail that the Savior said, "Peace, be still," to calm the wind and the waves. In all three accounts, the disciples were rebuked for their lack of faith, although the rebuking precedes the miracle only in Matthew's version. They all agree that the marvel of the miracle caused the disciples to respond in the same manner, exclaiming, "What manner of man is this, that even the winds and the sea obey him!"

Matthew 8:

23 And when he was entered into a ship, his disciples followed him.

24 And, behold, there arose a great tempest in the sea, insomuch that the ship was covered with the waves: but he was asleep.

25 And his disciples came to him, and awoke him, saying, Lord, save us: we perish.

26 And he saith unto them, Why are ye fearful, O ye of little faith? Then he arose, and rebuked the winds and the sea; and there was a great calm.

27 But the men marvelled, saying, What manner of man is this, that even the winds and the sea obey him!

Mark 4:

36 And when they had sent away the multitude, they took him even as he was in the ship. And there were also with him other little ships.

37 And there arose a great storm of wind, and the waves beat into the ship, so that it was now full.

38 And he was in the hinder part of the ship, asleep on a pillow: and they awake him, and say unto him, Master, carest thou not that we perish?

39 And he arose, and rebuked the wind, and said unto the sea, Peace, be still. And the wind ceased, and there was a great calm.

40 And he said unto them, Why are ye so fearful? how is it that ye have no faith?

41 And they feared exceedingly, and said one to another, What manner of man is this, that even the wind and the sea obey him?

Luke 8:

22 Now it came to pass on a certain day, that he went into a ship with his disciples: and he said unto them, Let us go over unto the other side of the lake. And they launched forth.

23 But as they sailed he fell asleep: and there came down a storm of wind on the lake; and they were filled with water, and were in jeopardy.
24 And they came to him, and awoke him, saying, Master, master, we perish. Then he arose, and rebuked the wind and the raging of the water: and they ceased, and there was a calm.
25 And he said unto them, Where is your faith? And they being afraid wondered, saying one to another, What manner of man is this! for he commandeth even the winds and water, and they obey him.

The other occurrence, detailed both in chapters 6 of Mark and John, describes the disciples in ships on the sea initially in the absence of the Savior. However, the Savior recognizes their plight and walks out on the water to them. In both accounts, the Savior previously departed to a mountain, and Mark adds the detail that the purpose was so the Savior could pray. The wind arose and caused the sea waves to rise. In both accounts, they saw someone walking toward them on the water, and the disciples, not recognizing the Savior, were frightened. After telling them to be not afraid, the Savior calmed the winds and waves.

Mark 6:
45 And straightway he constrained his disciples to get into the ship, and to go to the other side before unto Bethsaida, while he sent away the people.
46 And when he had sent them away, he departed into a mountain to pray.
47 And when even was come, the ship was in the midst of the sea, and he alone on the land.
48 And he saw them toiling in rowing; for the wind was contrary unto them: and about the fourth watch of the night he cometh unto them, walking upon the sea, and would have passed by them.

49 But when they saw him walking upon the sea, they supposed it had been a spirit, and cried out:

50 For they all saw him, and were troubled. And immediately he talked with them, and saith unto them, Be of good cheer: it is I; be not afraid.

51 And he went up unto them into the ship; and the wind ceased: and they were sore amazed in themselves beyond measure, and wondered.

John 6:

15 When Jesus therefore perceived that they would come and take him by force, to make him a king, he departed again into a mountain himself alone.

16 And when even was now come, his disciples went down unto the sea,

17 And entered into a ship, and went over the sea toward Capernaum. And it was now dark, and Jesus was not come to them.

18 And the sea arose by reason of a great wind that blew.

19 So when they had rowed about five and twenty or thirty furlongs, they see Jesus walking on the sea, and drawing nigh unto the ship: and they were afraid.

20 But he saith unto them, It is I; be not afraid.

21 Then they willingly received him into the ship: and immediately the ship was at the land whither they went.

The Miracle of Wind

As a riddle goes, "What is all about, but cannot be seen, can be captured, but cannot be held, has no throat, but can be heard?" The answer is wind.

Wind is the movement of air across the earth's surface caused by a difference in air pressure. Air from higher-pressure areas moves toward areas with lower pressure. The greater the pressure difference, the greater the speed at which wind travels. This pressure difference is created by the uneven heating of the earth's surface. On a global scale, as the sun heats the earth near the equator, the warm air and evaporated water vapor rise upward while the cool air from the poles moves to fill the empty space. Storm fronts occur when cool air from the poles meets warm, wet air from the equator. However, the wind doesn't typically blow north to south but rather in east-to-west directions. This phenomenon, known as the Coriolis effect, occurs because of the simultaneous rotation of the earth on its axis. This rotation additionally causes storm fronts in the northern hemisphere to rotate counterclockwise and storms in the southern hemisphere to rotate clockwise. On a more local scale, the uneven heating of the earth's surface can also lead to summer breezes near mountain ranges as cooler air from the mountains rushes down the canyon to replace the valley air that rises as it warms.

The earth contains five major wind zones: polar easterlies, westerlies, horse latitudes, trade winds, and the doldrums. The polar easterlies are dry-pressure systems located around the north and south poles. The westerlies receive high-pressure wind from the polar easterlies. The horse latitudes are strongest in the southern latitudes, where mountains that stop the wind are infrequent. This wind zone, therefore, is the primary driving force behind the most significant ocean current in the world, known as the Antarctic Circumpolar Current. Tradewinds are the most famous of the five major wind zones. Explorers used these reliable routes to travel east and west across the Atlantic Ocean between Europe and America. Most tropical storms, such as hurricanes, cyclones, or typhoons, develop from tradewinds as they converge on each other. The doldrum is located at the equator between 5 degrees north and south. Winds are famously calm or absent in this location, with breezes disappearing altogether, causing ships to get stuck for days or weeks. Tradewinds often cancel each other out in this persistent low-pressure zone.

Wind is a miracle of life. It is an essential component of the water cycle. Ocean water is heated by the sun, evaporates, and forms clouds of freshwater. Clouds carried by wind currents bring rainwater or snow to land in the form of precipitation. Rainwater refills aquifers, lakes, and streams. Snow becomes a storage of mountain water that slowly melts, providing a steady water source during warmer and drier periods. Wind is an essential part of plant life and growth. Plant seeds, pollen, and spores can be carried hundreds of miles across mountains and plains, bringing life to new areas. Wind creates strong ocean currents that circulate rich nutrients, oxygen, and food to maintain the abundant ocean life.

Wind power can be harnessed for many useful purposes. Trade winds moved ships and goods across the globe for hundreds of years. Wind patterns and velocity govern the development of airport runways and flight patterns in modern aerospace. Furthermore, understanding wind patterns at high altitudes allows jet pilots to travel in wind currents known as the "jet stream" to decrease fuel consumption and improve flight efficiency. Wind power is a formidable energy source that can turn wind turbines and convert energy into electricity. Wind patterns can be measured using Doppler radar (reflected sound waves off of weather systems), which helps predict weather patterns to warn people of impending storms.

The Miracle of Waves

You can't help but feel the grandeur of God and the universe as you look upward at the billions of stars on a clear night. In like manner, as you walk across the beach, it is hard to comprehend that the numbered posteriority of God's children is compared to the sands of the sea (Moses 1:28). Running your toes through the billions of sand grains while watching the endless blue waves come ashore against the backdrop of a never-ending blue sky is stunning. Although it may appear that the waves are carrying water from the ocean to the shore, ocean waves, before breaking, more accurately carry energy, not water. Waves result from energy passing through the water. Throw a rock in a still pond, and you can observe the energy of the rock entering the water converted into mini-rippled waves that travel in equal directions outward from the rock entrance. Although the wave travels outward, the actual water itself remains.

There are four types of ocean waves classified by their cause of origin. The most common type is known as wind waves. Wind encounters friction as it blows across the water's surface, and the energy creates waves. The waves are known as ocean swells when the wind is strong enough in the open ocean due to a major storm such as a hurricane. A third wave type, called tsunamis, can also be created by ice landslides, underwater volcanoes, or earthquakes. Finally, the fourth type of wave is called tidal wave. The moon's gravitational pull on the Earth creates these predictable waves.

Jesus Christ: The Creator

A quick scan of the topical guide reveals the many titles of Jesus. Some titles point to His mission, like "Savior," "Messiah," or "Lamb of God." Other titles give insight into his character, such as "Good Shepherd," "Prince of Peace," or "Wonderful." Some titles describe his attributes, such as "Bread of Life," "Light of the World," or the "Rock." Other titles describe his actions, like "Advocate," "Deliverer," or "Redeemer." Of particular importance to me is the title of "Creator."

The apostle John testified that "All things were made by him; and without him was not anything made that was made."[1] The prophet Joseph Smith proclaimed, "That by him, and through him, and of him, the worlds are and were created."[2] Through his voice he "Let the waters under the heaven be gathered together unto one place, and let the dry land appear: and it was so."[3] For the children of Israel trapped between the Red Sea and the approaching armies of Pharaoh, He "caused the sea to go back by a strong east wind all that night, and made the sea dry land, and the waters were divided and the children of Israel went into the sea upon dry ground: and the waters were a wall unto them on their right hand, and on their left."[4] As one who commanded the elements of wind and water from the very beginning and was able to do so again for the children of Israel, it should not come as a surprise that he would be able to command the wind and waves that were threatening to sink the ships of His disciples.

As the Creator, He can bring beauty instead of ashes.[5] He brought order to chaos as he organized the earth and the heavens. He is the master at creating something out of nothing. He can similarly create something out of nothing for each one of us who choose to follow Him.

President Nelson taught that when we turn to the Savior, we can have joy regardless of our circumstances. No matter how chaotic our lives may seem or how turbulent our current situation may appear, regardless of how discouraged we may feel because of what is happening or not happening in our lives, we can feel peace and joy by focusing on the Savior. He taught:

> "My dear brothers and sisters, the joy we feel has little to do with the circumstances of our lives and everything to do with the focus of our lives. When the focus of our lives is on God's plan of salvation... and Jesus Christ and His gospel, we can feel joy regardless of what is happening—or not happening—in our lives. Joy comes from and because of Him. He is the source of all joy."[6]

It is instructive that Mark specifies where Jesus was during the storm. He states that he was sleeping at the hinder part of the ship. The hinder part of the ship is the back of the boat where the rudder is located. The rudder is a small lever controlled by a helm to help steer the ship. In the book of James, we read,

> "Behold also the ships, which though they be so great, and are driven of fierce winds, yet are they turned about with a very small helm, whithersoever the governor listeth."[7]

In the Liberty Jail, the prophet Joseph Smith further emphasized this truth to the Saints.

> "You know, brethren, that a very large ship is benefited very much by a very small helm in the time of a storm, by being kept workways with the wind and the waves."[8]

When the storms of life arise, it is critical to our spiritual survival to have the Savior positioned in the center of our lives so he can steer and guide us. The purpose of doing so is not to avoid encountering stormy wind or waters. Trials and challenges are critical to our growth in becoming more like Him and our Heavenly Father. Sometimes, we recognize the hand of Jesus guiding us through the storm and bringing our ship safely to the other side. In other times, it may only be after we have sufficiently endured and thus gained experiential learning that the Savior will calm the wind and the seas. The account in Mark describes that the Savior saw them toiling in the stormy water, but it wasn't until the 4th watch that he decided to come out to help. The fourth watch of the night is between 3:00 am and 6:00 am. For some reason, the Lord saw fit to wait to save them with his grace after they had exhausted their best efforts.[9] Either way, the Savior can bring peace to the storm or our hearts as we weather the storm. Elder Ballard taught,

> "Please know that even though great storms of wind and waves beat upon the old ship, the Savior is on

board and is able to rebuke the storm with His command 'Peace, be still.' Until then, we must not fear, and we must have unwavering faith and know that "even the wind and the sea obey him."[10]

How can we position the Savior at the helm of our life? The prophet Jacob described the purpose in following the law of Moses: it "point[ed] our souls to Him and for this cause it is sanctified unto us for righteousness."[11] In the latter days, our covenants consist of baptism followed by covenants we make in the temple endowment to keep the laws of Obedience, Sacrifice, The Gospels, Chastity, and Consecration. These covenants point our souls to the Savior to receive His redemptive and enabling power to sanctify us unto righteousness. It may seem impossible that such a small thing as keeping our covenants can help us in the storms of life. However, just as it may seem unlikely that such a small rudder could control such a huge ship during the winds and waves of the sea, our covenants keep us safe and built us upon the rock of our Redeemer.[12]

When we make and keep temple covenants we are promised to be "endowed with power from on high."[13] Before becoming the prophet, President Nelson taught that "The greatest compliment that can be earned here in this life is to be known as a covenant keeper. The rewards for a covenant keeper will be realized both here and hereafter."[14] For this reason, President Nelson has repeatedly invited us to stay on the covenant path and to do everything we can to return to the covenant path if we have wandered. We are bound to the Savior when we make and keep covenants with God. Knowing this fact brings meaning to what the Savior taught.

> "These things I have spoken unto you, that in me ye might have peace. In the world ye shall have tribulation: but be of good cheer; I have overcome the world."[15]

He has overcome the world and its challenges, tribulations, and trials. When we bind ourselves to Him through our covenants, we will overcome the world with Him too! By allowing the Savior to be at the helm, he can guide us through the personal revelation we receive. President Nelson has pleaded with us to increase our spiritual capacity to receive personal revelation.

> "Our Savior and Redeemer, Jesus Christ, will perform some of His mightiest works between now and when He comes again. We will see miraculous indications that God the Father and His Son, Jesus Christ, preside over this Church in majesty and glory. But in coming days, it will not be possible to survive spiritually without the guiding, directing, comforting, and constant influence of the Holy Ghost. My beloved brothers and sisters, I plead with you to increase your spiritual capacity to receive revelation...Choose to do the spiritual work required to enjoy the gift of the Holy Ghost and hear the voice of the Spirit more frequently and more clearly."[16]

Reflection:
1. How has faith in the Lord Jesus Christ helped you through challenging times?
2. How can fully living your covenants help you through the storms of life?
3. What can you do to increase your spiritual capacity to receive revelation?

---

[1] John 1:3

[2] D&C 76:24

[3] Genesis 1:9

[4] Exodus 14:21-22

[5] Isaiah 61:3

[6] Russell M. Nelson. "Joy and Spiritual Survival," General Conference, October 2016

[7] James 3:4

[8] Doctrine and Covenants 123:16

[9] 2 Nephi 25:23

[10] M. Russell Ballard. "To Whom Shall We Go?" General Conference, October 2016

[11] Jacob 4:5

[12] Helaman 5:12

[13] Joseph Smith Papers, 1831

[14] Russell M. Nelson. "Covenants," General Conference, October 2011

[15] John 16:33

[16] Russell M. Nelson. "Revelation for the Church. Revelation for Our Lives," General Conference, April 2018

Chapter 9

Jesus Heals the Woman with an Issue of Blood

Jesus had recently called Matthew, a despised tax collector, to be one of his disciples. As He and His disciples sat down to eat, the Pharisees criticized Jesus' actions. They condemned that he was associating with publicans - despised Jews who worked for the Roman government to collect taxes and were considered traitors - in addition to eating with people judged to be "sinners." In parables, Jesus taught that his mission was not to call the righteous to repentance, but sinners to repentance, for "they that be whole need not a physician, but they that are sick."[1] Between healing the leper, the febrile, the paralytic, or bringing the dead back to life, Jesus had already established himself as the master physician. However, this reference to a physician additionally foreshadows what is about to take place as he heals a woman with an issue of blood.

The setting for this miracle was a large crowd pressing forward to see and follow the Savior. At His meal, He was asked by Jarius, the leader of a synagogue, to come quickly to his house to heal his dying 12-year-old daughter, according to Luke's account. However, Matthew's account states the daughter was now dead. In an attempt to travel to Jarius's daughter, he was met by crowds of people. One of the people in the crowd was a woman with "an issue of blood" for over 12 years. Despite spending all she had earned to seek help from physicians who were unable to heal her, she continued to suffer. Her healing is documented in three of the four gospels - Matthew, Mark, and Luke - suggesting its importance.

In all accounts, the woman came from behind the Savior and touched the border (Luke) or hem (Matthew) of the Savior's garment. In Matthew and Mark, we learn that the woman had thought within herself that this simple act would allow her to be made whole. Matthew's account is the shortest and differs by stating that the Savior turned immediately to her, and she was made whole from that hour. In Luke and Mark's accounts, we get more detail that she had spent all her wages seeking healing from physicians to no avail. She was immediately healed upon touching the Savior's garment, and the bleeding instantly dried up.

Jesus then, sensing that someone had touched Him because he felt that virtue or, in other words, power had left him, inquired who touched him. His disciples considered this a silly question because there were so many people that it would be impossible to know who did this. The woman feared what might happen if she was discovered to be the person but, at the same time, knew that she was now healed. She bowed before the Savior and confessed to touching the Savior's garment. She also testified of her healing. In both accounts, the Savior credits the woman's faith as the reason for her healing. The following are the accounts in Matthew, Luke, and Mark.

> Matthew 9:
> 20 And, behold, a woman, which was diseased with an issue of blood twelve years, came behind him, and touched the hem of his garment:
> 21 For she said within herself, If I may but touch his garment, I shall be whole.
> 22 But Jesus turned him about, and when he saw her, he said, Daughter, be of good comfort; thy faith hath made thee whole. And the woman was made whole from that hour.
>
> Luke 8:
> 43. And a woman having an issue of blood twelve years, which had spent all her living upon physicians, neither could be healed of any,
> 44 Came behind him, and touched the border of his garment: and immediately her issue of blood stanched.

45 And Jesus said, Who touched me? When all denied, Peter and they that were with him said, Master, the multitude throng thee and press thee, and sayest thou, Who touched me?

46 And Jesus said, Somebody hath touched me: for I perceive that virtue is gone out of me.

47 And when the woman saw that she was not hid, she came trembling, and falling down before him, she declared unto him before all the people for what cause she had touched him, and how she was healed immediately.

48 And he said unto her, Daughter, be of good comfort: thy faith hath made thee whole; go in peace.

Mark 5:

24 And Jesus went with him; and much people followed him, and thronged him.

25 And a certain woman, which had an issue of blood twelve years,

26 And had suffered many things of many physicians, and had spent all that she had, and was nothing bettered, but rather grew worse,

27 When she had heard of Jesus, came in the press behind, and touched his garment.

28 For she said, If I may touch but his clothes, I shall be whole.

29 And straightway the fountain of her blood was dried up; and she felt in her body that she was healed of that plague.

30 And Jesus, immediately knowing in himself that virtue had gone out of him, turned him about in the press, and said, Who touched my clothes?

31 And his disciples said unto him, Thou seest the multitude thronging thee, and sayest thou, Who touched me?

32 And he looked round about to see her that had done this thing.

33 But the woman fearing and trembling, knowing what was done in her, came and fell down before him, and told him all the truth.

34 And he said unto her, Daughter, thy faith hath made thee whole; go in peace, and be whole of thy plague.

The Miracle of Blood: Hemostasis

Hemostasis is the delicate balance between proteins in the blood that make blood clots when tissue injury occurs and dissolving or preventing inappropriate clots when formed. The ultimate goal is to ensure that blood properly circulates to deliver oxygen from the lungs to the individual cells. If an imbalance toward clot formation (thrombosis) occurs, then problems with oxygen delivery can occur. Thrombosis in the arteries of the heart can cause a heart attack. Thrombosis in the vessels of the brain can cause a stroke. Clots that can develop in the leg's deep veins (deep vein thrombosis or DVT) can propagate or break off and travel to the lungs resulting in a pulmonary embolism (PE). If any of these occur, it can cause massive disability or death. If blood protein balance is tipped toward preventing clot formation or toward dissolving properly formed clots when injury occurs, then catastrophic bleeding can occur. Inappropriate or excessive bleeding in the gastrointestinal tract or following an injury, unfortunately, occasionally results when medications are used to either inactivate proteins responsible for clot formation or to promote clot dissolution (thrombolysis), in other words "thin the blood," in people with history of, or genetic predisposition to, inappropriate clot formation. An unfortunate side effect of treating people with "blood thinners" to treat or prevent heart attack, stroke, or DVT/PE is unintended bleeding.

When the vessels of your circulatory system are injured either externally (i.e. injury or surgery) or internally (often due to vessel inflammation such as high cholesterol causing vessel weakening and making them prone to shear stress from high blood pressure), the process to prevent bleeding is known as primary hemostasis. Platelets are a component of blood that circulate and stick to von Willebrand Factor (vWF) or Tissue Factor (TF), cellular proteins that are present in damaged cells. This interaction causes platelets to become activated. Activated platelets change their shape to create a plug to stop the bleeding and release calcium, thromboxane, and other chemicals that cause other platelets nearby to also become sticky. Creating sticky platelets is known as the coagulation cascade. It is characterized as an intrinsic pathway (originating from damaged surfaces of the inside of the vessels) or an extrinsic pathway (originating from external cuts or trauma). The proteins involved in each pathway have Roman numeral designations. In the intrinsic pathway, factor XII is converted to XIIa ("a" stands for "activated"), which then is an enzyme to activate factor XI to ultimately create Xa, the enzyme responsible for converting prothrombin into thrombin. In the extrinsic pathway, trauma causes factor VII to be activated, which then, in the presence of tissue factor, activates factor Xa, which then activates thrombin. Thrombin's purpose is to convert fibrinogen to fibrin, a protein that links activated platelets together. Fibrin linking activated platelets together a process known as secondary hemostasis. If platelets are like bricks, then fibrin is like the mortar that holds the structure together.

    To only form clots at the site of injury, some proteins are simultaneously activated to turn off the process. This helps prevent clots from rapidly growing on the inside surface of damaged vessels and inadvertently blocking the entire vessel. It also stabilizes good clots and prevents them from breaking off and traveling elsewhere. Once the bleeding stops with the platelet plug and fibrin cross links, the body will work on repairing the damaged tissue, dissolving the clot (thrombolysis), and replacing the clot with repaired tissue.

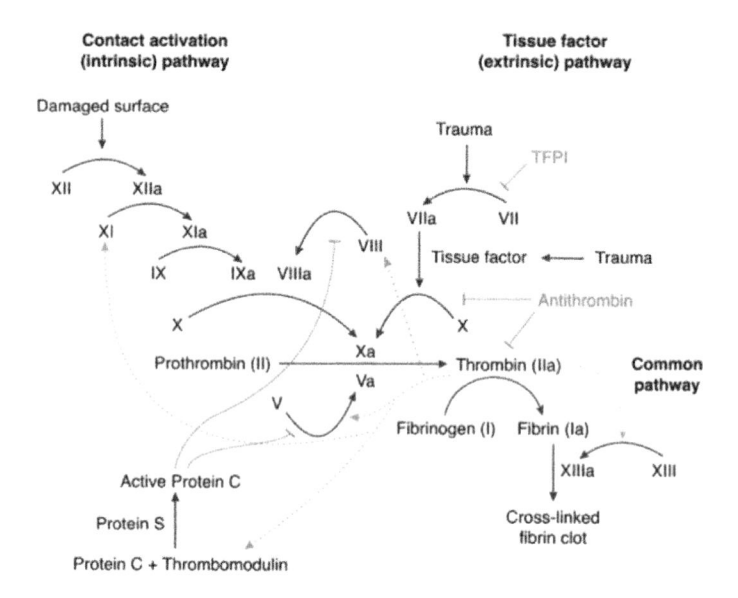

```
                Contact activation                    Tissue factor
                (intrinsic) pathway                   (extrinsic) pathway
        Damaged surface
               ↓                              Trauma
                                                ↓      TFPI
         XII      XIIa                                ↙
                                           VIIa      VII
           XI     XIa          VIII
                          ↙          Tissue factor ← Trauma
              IX    IXa  VIIIa
                                                  ⊢——— Antithrombin
               X                        X
                              Xa
              Prothrombin (II) ———→ Thrombin (IIa)    Common
                              Va                       pathway
                        V
                              Fibrinogen (I)  Fibrin (Ia)
                                                  │ XIIIa    XIII
             Active Protein C
                    ↑                           Cross-linked
               Protein S                         fibrin clot
                    │
           Protein C + Thrombomodulin
```

The diagram below shows the pro-thrombotic and anti-clot pathways.

Issue of Blood: Hemostatic Imbalance

Given the complexity of homeostasis, it is not surprising that many genetic variations can lead the balance to tip and become either prothrombotic or prone to bleeding. Furthermore, the myriad of enzymes and proteins involved in both systems have become the target of multiple medications to correct system imbalances. For example, individuals may inherit genetic changes in the Factor V protein (Factor V Leiden) that make it harder for Protein C to inhibit its proclotting activity. Deficiencies in Protein S, Protein C, or Antithrombin (proteins responsible for inhibiting the activation of Factor V or X) also result in increased clot formation. People with such genetic variations may require medications that inhibit thrombin (direct thrombin inhibitors) or Xa (heparin or enoxaparin) activity to prevent inappropriate clot formation. Furthermore, people with a history of heart disease or stroke may take medications such as clopidogrel (Plavix) or aspirin to inhibit platelet activation so that platelets don't inappropriately plug up narrowed and calcified vessels of the heart or brain. If clots in the brain or lung do form, treatment with systemic or local TPA (tissue plasminogen factor) can dissolve the connective fibrin links that hold the activated platelets together, break apart the clot, and restore blood flow and oxygen delivery to the body.

In contrast, some people may have deficiencies or mutations in vWF (von Willebrand's disease), factor VIII (hemophilia A), or factor IX (hemophilia B), making them prone to bleeding when injured. Similarly, if treatment for pro-clot conditions causes the blood to be "too thin", such individuals may have trouble forming clots when necessary; their proteins are non-functional. Therefore, they may need to receive plasma, platelets, or other blood proteins to stop bleeding. The fact that, for the most part, when we injure ourselves, we don't bleed to death or form massive life-threatening blood clots is truly a miracle. Furthermore, it is truly a miracle that despite coagulation's complexity, we can often diagnose and treat homeostasis imbalance with targeted medications and blood products.

This diagnosis is often required when patients come into the hospital after experiencing trauma. Frequently, the severity of bleeding requires blood transfusions during or immediately after transport to the emergency department. During blood loss and replacement, deficiencies in key components of primary and secondary hemostasis often occur. Obtaining a study called a thromboelastogram (TEG) can be very helpful. A TEG study measures the resistance to a small filament as it moves in the blood that is trying to clot. Based on the time it takes to form a clot, the strength of that clot, and whether the clot breaks down over time, physicians can pinpoint whether a patient has sufficient coagulation factors (the time it takes to start forming a clot or R time), fibrinogen (the time it takes to reach a fixed strength or K time), platelets and fibrinogen crosslinks (the speed or alpha angle at which it takes to reach maximum clot strength or MA), and whether any excess fibrinolysis is occurring (the time it takes for the clot to begin to degrade). A knowledge of the patient's medical history and medications, in combination with any abnormal TEG values, can point to a specific treatment.

Although it is not exactly clear the cause of the woman's issue of blood, the footnote in Mark and Matthew states it was hemorrhage, which further supports that her healing was manifest in her "fountain of blood dr[ying] up." Given that the cross reference of the word blood directs to Leviticus chapter 15, where it outlines the various discharges of bodily fluids and the time and required procedures for one to become clean again, it is likely that society ostracized this woman for the last twelve years.   It is possible that she may had deficiencies in various clotting proteins and components of hemostasis.

However, given the cross-reference to Leviticus, it is more likely that she had persistent uterine bleeding either from persistent menstruation or abnormal uterine bleeding from conditions such as thickened uterine endometrium or a uterine fibroid. Modern treatment options include oral contraceptives to adjust hormonal imbalances, hysteroscopy and thermal ablation to cauterize the uterine lining, dilation and curettage to remove retained products of conception, interventional radiology coiling of uterine blood vessels, surgical myomectomy (removal of uterine fibroid) or a hysterectomy (removing the uterus) to stop persistent uterine bleeding.

Although it is unclear how much blood she had lost over the last twelve years, the fact that she was able to make her way through the crowds on foot suggests it was slow enough that she didn't have symptoms of major blood loss and that likely her body was sufficiently able to keep up with blood production equal to the rate of her loss. However, according to Leviticus, she and everything and everyone she touched would be considered unclean while she was experiencing this "issue of blood". It took a considerable act of faith to venture out in a public setting, and she likely appreciated the anonymity the crowd afforded her. She demonstrates that faith in the Lord Jesus Christ was more than a belief but a principle of action, and she, therefore, accepted the risk that she would make the Savior's garment unclean by her touch, having faith that He could heal her.

Principled Balance

Maintaining a balance between clot formation and clot dissolution is essential to our circulatory system. If the system is out of balance favoring either process, devastating consequences can occur. Equal emphasis needs to be placed by the body on each system to function optimally. In like manner, the gospel is full of equally important principles that may appear paradoxical on the surface but are, in fact, essential virtues that one must simultaneously apply in balance. Examples include justice and mercy or grace, love and law, faith and works, spirituality and religiosity. God is full of justice and yet also mercy and grace. He embodies and reflects both perfectly. God is Love,[2] but God can not violate His own laws, or else he would cease to be God.[3] "Salvation comes unto the children of men through faith on His name,"[4] but we must "Work out [our] own salvation with fear and trembling."[5]

An overemphasis on His mercy might lead one to erroneously believe that it doesn't matter how one uses their agency, for even if "God beats us with a few stripes we shall be saved in the Kingdom of God."[6] However, if we ignore His grace, we may lose hope, feeling that we can't return to His presence because of His strict declaration that "no unclean thing can enter the kingdom of heaven."[7] And, despite our best efforts we all sin and fall short of the glory of God.[8]

The prophet Joseph Smith taught, "By proving contraries, truth is made manifest."[9] Brigham Young similarly taught:

"All facts are proved and made manifest by their opposite."[10] As one attempts to find the right balance, it becomes clear that Jesus Christ is the perfect example of one who applies seemingly contradictory virtues equally. Just as He was the answer to finding hemostasis (balance in the blood clotting and blood circulation) in the woman with an issue of blood, he is the answer to balancing every good thing. Alma taught that God is merciful because of Jesus Christ, and through Him, God has fulfilled the demands of justice, thus allowing God to be both just and merciful.[11] The prophet Joseph Smith taught that we believe all humankind may be saved by obedience to the laws and ordinances of the gospel through what? The atonement of Jesus Christ.[12] James taught that faith without works is dead.[13] However, we are not saved by our works. Instead, we are saved by grace.[14] By whose grace? The grace of Jesus Christ purchased us with His shedding of blood in the Garden of Gethsemane and on the cross of Calvary so that we may not suffer if we repent.[15]

As we follow Jesus Christ, we often face competing choices for our time, attention, and energy. We are commanded to be in the world but not of the world. We need to develop our spirituality (our inner relationship with God) and fine-tune our religiosity (our outward interaction with others as we worship). We are commanded to simultaneously love God and our neighbor, regardless of whether we feel our neighbor deserves to be loved.

Regarding these two great commandments on which hang all the law and prophets, Christ teaches us how to balance where we devote our time, energy, and love. We risk error if we profess dedication to God through scrupulous scripture reading, prayer, and gospel study but ignore serving our neighbors in need as we pass by, like the priest in the parable of the good Samaritan. In contrast, if we neglect to develop our vertical relationship with God through prayer, scripture reading, and daily repentance, then our power to perceive and meet the needs of our fellow beings will diminish. It is incorrect to assume that being social (developing our relationship with our fellowmen) and spiritual (developing our relationship with God) are competing interests. Indeed, the Savior himself taught "If you love me, feed my sheep."[16] Even the earliest accounts of the Savior as a twelve-year-old boy demonstrate that he was going about His Father's business by being among the people at the temple. In summary, loving God means serving and loving your neighbor. Furthermore, King Benjamin taught that "when ye are in the services of your fellow beings, ye are only in the service of your God."[17] In short, loving your neighbor is a primary way to show love to God.

Jared Halverson, an institute teacher and gospel scholar, points out that these two great commandments were not only repeatedly taught by the Savior but can be embodied in the symbolism of His cross.

> "I often hear the phrase, 'I'm spiritual but not religious.' I get that! Being spiritual is about connecting with God. It's the vertical dimension of our discipleship, the first great commandment (loving God with all our heart, might, mind, and strength). But not being able to "go to church [during the pandemic]" has shown me even more clearly the importance of being "religious" as well. And that doesn't mean just making my meetings; it means making meaningful connections while I'm there—with others, and with God through others—the serving-God-while-serving-others kinds of connections that King Benjamin had in mind. It's the horizontal dimension of our discipleship, the second great commandment (loving our neighbor as ourselves). And those two elements—the spiritual and the social—are both essential. Although we don't use the cross in our symbolism, it's a beautiful metaphor for what it looks like when those two elements are firmly attached—the vertical and the horizontal—

crossbeams meant to manifest the ultimate love of God."[18]

The more we learn of the Savior - his life, actions, and attributes - the more desire we will have to apply His teachings in our lives. We will begin to not just know about the Savior but truly know Him. Trust Him. Believe Him. He will bring harmony and unity to the paradoxes of life. That is the essence of the atonement, or "at-one-ment." The atonement brings together seemingly opposing virtues into unity. We will realize that faith in Him is not a passive belief but a principle of action, and therefore, obedience to his gospel is a simultaneous demonstration of faith and works. We will realize that the time we devote to loving and serving our family, friends, neighbors, fellow church members in our callings, and even our enemies is how we demonstrate our devotion to God. We will find that the purpose of God's law is not to inflict deserved punishment and suffering when we make mistakes, but instead, the purpose of the law is to show love and to judge what is needed to "relieve suffering and liberate sinners."[19]

Consider how the Savior perfectly applied love and law when the woman caught in adultery was brought to Him.[20] Although the law states that she should be stoned, He lovingly said that "he who is without sin cast the first stone."[21] When her accusers left, He lovingly encouraged her to go her way and sin no more.[22] He applied the higher love the law required - to do what good was needed for her to become better instead of doing what others think she may have deserved. Adam Miller teaches that "God's justice and grace are intertwined." That "justice is the work of saving people from evil - both the evil they suffer and the evil they do."[23] He explains,

> "Grace is the art of giving good for good and good for evil. Grace is the art of giving whatever good is needed. And if justice is the art of giving whatever good is needed - and not, indeed, the business of giving

only what's deserved - then justice and grace are two names for the same thing."[24]

Reflection:
1. Consider how your thoughts, behaviors, and actions show your love toward God. What is one thing you can work on now to improve your connection and relationship with God?
2. What is one thing that you can do to cultivate meaningful relationships with those around you, and how can you more fully live the second great command of "loving your neighbor as yourself."
3. With the direction of the spirit, are there any changes you need to make in how you spend your time and energy to devote more time to serving God and your fellow man?

---

[1] Matthew 9:12-13

[2] 1 John 4:8

[3] Alma 42:24-25

[4] Mosiah 3:9

[5] Philippians 2:12

[6] 2 Nephi 28:8

[7] 1 Nephi 15:34

[8] Romans 3:23

[9] Joseph Smith, History of the Church, 6:428

[10] Brigham Young, Discourses of Brigham Young, sel. John A. Widtsoe [1954], 433

[11] Alma 33:11-12

[12] Article of faith 3

[13] James 2:17-18

[14] 2 Nephi 25:23

[15] Doctrine and Covenants 18:10-13

[16] John 21:15-17

[17] Mosiah 2:17

[18] Jared Halverson. "Why Home-Church and Church-Church Need Each Other." LDS Living, May 6, 2020

[19] Miller, Adam. Original Grace, page 35

[20] John 8:4

[21] John 8:7

[22] John 8:11

[23] Miller, Adam. Original Grace, page 40

[24] Miller, Adam. Original Grace, page 41

Chapter 10
Jesus Heals the Blind

On four separate occasions and in three of the four gospels - Matthew, Mark, and John - Jesus performs the miracle of healing the blind. On two of these occasions, both in the Gospel of Matthew, two blind men come to the Savior asking for healing. In both instances, the two men cried out for mercy to Jesus, identifying him as the Son of David. In Matthew chapter 9, Jesus first inquires, "Believe ye that I am able to do this?" and heals according to their faith. In chapter 20, the second account, He initially asks the two blind men what they would have Him do for them. In these two separate accounts, Jesus touched their eyes to heal them. Upon doing so, Matthew 9 states that "their eyes were opened," whereas in Matthew 20, the blind men "received their sight immediately."

Matthew 9: 27-31

> 27 And when Jesus departed thence, two blind men followed him, crying, and saying, Thou Son of David, have mercy on us.
> 28 And when he was come into the house, the blind men came to him: and Jesus saith unto them, Believe ye that I am able to do this? They said unto him, Yea, Lord.
> 29 Then touched he their eyes, saying, According to your faith be it unto you.
> 30 And their eyes were opened; and Jesus straitly charged them, saying, See that no man know it.
> 31 But they, when they were departed, spread broad his fame in all that country.

Matthew 20: 27-31

30 And, behold, two blind men sitting by the way side, when they heard that Jesus passed by, cried out, saying, Have mercy on us, O Lord, thou Son of David.

31 And the multitude rebuked them, because they should hold their peace: but they cried the more, saying, Have mercy on us, O Lord, thou Son of David.

32 And Jesus stood still, and called them, and said, What will ye that I shall do unto you?

33 They say unto him, Lord, that our eyes may be opened.

34 So Jesus had compassion on them, and touched their eyes: and immediately their eyes received sight, and they followed him.

The third account of visual healing in the gospel of Mark is quite different. People brought the blind man to Jesus and requested healing, as in Matthew's other two accounts. In Mark, Jesus took the blind man outside the town, spit on his eyes, and then asked him what he saw. The man reports seeing figures he describes as "men as trees walking." Jesus then placed his hands on the blind man's eyes again and commanded him to look up, and after doing so, the blind man could now see every man clearly.

Mark 8:22-26

22 And he cometh to Bethsaida; and they bring a blind man unto him, and besought him to touch him.

23 And he took the blind man by the hand, and led him out of the town; and when he had spit on his eyes, and put his hands upon him, he asked him if he saw ought.

24 And he looked up, and said, I see men as trees, walking.

25 After that he put his hands again upon his eyes, and made him look up: and he was restored, and saw <u>every man</u> clearly.

26 And he sent him away to his house, saying, Neither go into the town, nor tell it to any in the town.

The fourth account of healing from blindness is described in the gospel of John and occurred after the disciples asked Jesus a question about the blind man. Upon seeing the blind man, the disciples inquired if the cause of his blindness was sin from either the blind man or the blind man's parents. Jesus debunked the assumption that the root of his blindness was due to sin, but instead exists so "that the works of God could be manifest in this man." Without him even asking for a miracle or Jesus testing this man's belief or faith as had occurred with the previous three accounts, Jesus once again spat on the ground, created a clay that he used to anoint the blind man's eyes, and instructed him to wash in the pool of Siloam. The man received his sight and testified simply of what Jesus asked him to do and how he received his vision. The Pharisees, who were skeptical of the miracle, repeatedly accused the man and his parents of lying about not being able to see since birth. They cast the blind man out after he and his parents wouldn't fall victim to the trap the Pharisees were attempting to catch them in regarding Christ, God, and the Sabbath. Jesus went and found the blind man and testified to him that he was the Son of God. The blind man believed in the Savior's words and worshiped Him.

John 9:1-7 (for complete account, read all of chapter 9)
1 And as Jesus passed by, he saw a man which was blind from his birth.
2 And his disciples asked him, saying, Master, who did sin, this man, or his parents, that he was born blind?
3 Jesus answered, Neither hath this man sinned, nor his parents: but that the works of God should be made manifest in him.
4 I must work the works of him that sent me, while it is day: the night cometh, when no man can work.

5 As long as I am in the world, I am the light of the world.

6 When he had thus spoken, he spat on the ground, and made clay of the spittle, and he anointed the eyes of the blind man with the clay,

7 And said unto him, Go, wash in the pool of Siloam, (which is by interpretation, Sent.) He went his way therefore, and washed, and came seeing.

The Miracle of Vision

Living in the foothills of the Rocky Mountains, I'm fortunate to experience the beauty of the earth that the four seasons offer. Spring's lush green grass growing grand on the mountainside graces my legs as I trail run and then morph into fields of gold as the summer season settles. Splendorous summer sunsets burst from the sky, scattering vivid purple, pink, and burnt red-orange rays as the sun drops behind the western mountains each evening. As the warm breeze of morning transforms into a crisp chill of autumn, yellow aspens and fire-red scrub oaks pop up in the canyons. Falling leaves change to fallen snow as winter commences, and the peace of the moon's light reflects upon Earth's fresh white blanket as she slumbers until spring awakens her again with blossoming flowers.

> For the beauty of the earth,
> For the beauty of the skies,
> For the love which from our birth
> Over and around us lies,
>
> For the beauty of each hour
> Of the day and of the night,
> Hill and vale, and tree and flow'r,
> Sun and moon, and stars of light,

> Lord of all, to thee we raise
> This our hymn of grateful praise.[1]

The imagery of each season is beautiful to experience, and it is all possible because of the miracle of sight.

Alma taught that "all things denote there is a God; yea even the earth, and all things that are upon the face of it."[2] Despite evidence all around us, the Savior teaches that many people remain with their eyes closed to the things of God but blessed is one that has eyes to see.[3] Regarding our visual world and its relation to the things of God, perhaps C.S. Lewis said it best. "I believe in Christ like I believe in the sun. Not because I can see it, but by it I can see everything else."[4] Indeed, the light of Christ is in everything, and due to the miracle of sight, we can see everything because of Him. The light of Christ, which is in all things and gives light to all things,[5] is integral to the miracle of sight.

Making sense of the visual world is truly a miracle. Sight is created by light waves that reflect off objects around us. Depending on the color and material of the object, the beams of energy are either partially absorbed or reflected. Things we identify as the color green absorb all other wavelengths of light on the visual spectrum but reflect to our eyes energy at a wavelength on this spectrum that we consider to be green in color.

When light strikes an object, the object absorbs some wavelengths of light while others are reflected. The reflected wavelengths travel toward our eye and enter the eye's outermost surface, called the cornea. The cornea bends the light coming in at all angles through the pupil and focuses it through the lens to the back of the retina. The pupil is the dark-colored center of our eye, surrounded by the pigmented iris. The iris works like a camera shutter that can expand or contract to regulate the volume of light allowed to enter. In low-level light conditions, the iris thins to enlarge the pupil and let in more light through the eye to improve clarity of vision. When ample light is shining on the eye, the iris constricts and limits the amount of light that enters. The light passes through the cornea and pupil through the lens suspended by ciliary muscles that can expand or contract to bend the lens. The eye lens functions similarly to the lens of a camera to focus on objects near or far.

Light refracted by the cornea and focused by the lens then passes through a gelatin-like substance called the vitreous until it strikes the back of the retina, activating specialized nerves that take each wavelength and convert it into electric nerve impulses that travel along the optic nerve to the brain. The two specialized nerve cells in the retina are rods and cones. Cones are the primary photo nerve cells concentrated at the central retina and responsible for detailed vision and color. Conversely, rods are located at the periphery, have lower acuity, and are primarily responsible for night vision. Even though about 12 million rod and 6 million cone cells are located on the retina, each cone makes a single connection with the optic nerve, whereas multiple rods converge to connect to one nerve cell. This accounts for the rod's lower acuity. When an image comes through the cornea and lens, it is inverted through the vitreous before it strikes the back of the retina. As the electrical impulse travels along the optic nerve into the back of the brain, the visual cortex of the occipital lobe inverts the image back so that our minds interpret the image correctly.

Although the vision capability of one eye is miraculous, even more so is the process our two eyes use to work. For example, light that strikes the retina on the medial side (close to the nose) travels along the optic nerve but then crosses at the optic chiasm to enter the other side of the brain. These nerves join the nerves processing the light that strikes the other eye's lateral retina (ear side) as these nerve fibers enter the brain on the same side (red visual field and red optic tract). It all has to do with angles. When light comes in from the right side of the body, it travels toward the medial part of the right eye and the lateral part of the left eye. As these waves activate the retinal photocells and begin to travel along the optic nerve, the brain can receive part of the information from the right eye as the nerves cross the optic chiasm and join it with nerve impulses the brain is receiving from the nerve cells of the lateral left eye. The visual input is combined to form a more complete picture. This is helpful because, given the nose's position, the left eye's medial side is obscured from receiving light reflecting off images to the observer's right side.

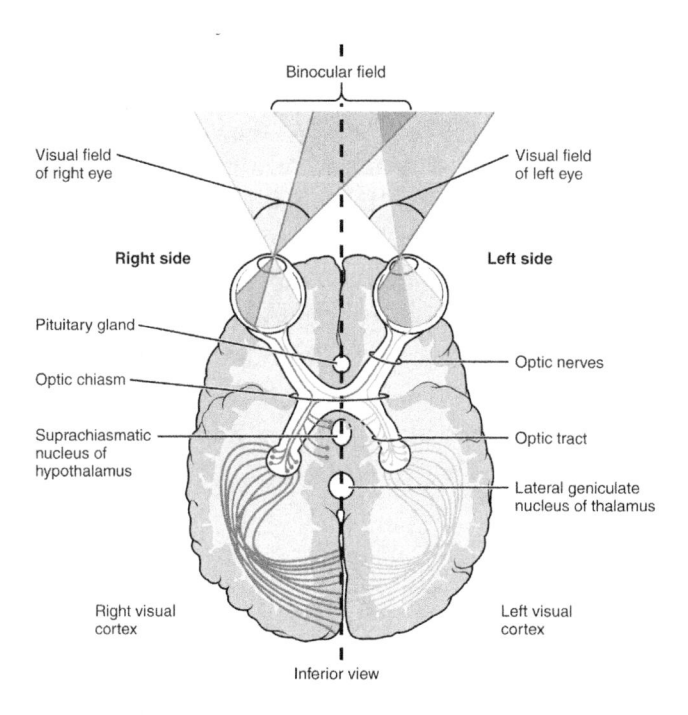

Binocular field

Visual field of right eye

Visual field of left eye

Right side

Left side

Pituitary gland

Optic nerves

Optic chiasm

Suprachiasmatic nucleus of hypothalamus

Optic tract

Lateral geniculate nucleus of thalamus

Right visual cortex

Left visual cortex

Inferior view

Two eyes help form a complete picture in our brain and allow us to determine depth perception due to the overlap between both right and left visual fields (binocular field). With two eyes positioned approximately 2 inches apart, each eye receives wavelengths of light from slightly different angles. When the brain compares the two pictures, it can create depth perception. Based on the angle of how two objects reflect light into one eye versus another, the brain can determine which object is closer and the relative distances between objects.

The ability to see and comprehend the visual world only happens in stages. Human vision takes nearly a year to develop fully after birth. When babies are first born, their retinas are still developing, and the pupils are small, limiting the light they receive. Eyeball muscles take a few weeks to strengthen through independent, uncoordinated movements until a baby can hold the eye stationary and project an image on the retina. At this stage in development, the pupils widen, the retina receives more light, and infants begin to see large objects, colors, and shapes. However, because rods and cones are still developing, visual acuity ranges between 20/200 and 20/800 up to the first month. At about one month, they can focus briefly on objects as their acuity improves to 20/150 and then eventually 20/20 at age six months. However, it isn't until about 2-4 months before their eyes work together to track moving objects coordinately. This coordination leads to depth perception, and babies reach for things as they see the world in three dimensions. They begin to discern the closeness of objects sometime between months 5-8.

Blindness

Any disruption along the visual pathway from the cornea to the brain may result in partial vision loss or blindness. The cause of vision loss is typically categorized into three anatomical groups: media, retina, and neuronal.

Media causes of vision loss include corneal, anterior chamber, lens, and posterior chamber conditions. A sudden or persistent opacification of the corneal surface can occur due to trauma or infection. The result prevents light waves from entering the eye. The cornea comprises a thin layer layer (5-7 cells) of epithelium (skin) that rests on top of a connective tissue. This connective tissue stromal layer accounts for 80-85% of the corneal thickness. Stromal collagen fibers provide the cornea's strength, structure, transparency, and refraction capability. Nutrients to maintain and heal the cornea pass from the anterior chamber through a posterior corneal membrane into the stroma. Infection or trauma of the cornea may result in scar formation that prevents light from correctly entering the eye. A corneal transplant can restore light refraction and light passage through the eye if severely damaged. Blood in the anterior chamber between the cornea and the lens, known as a hyphema, can permanently stain the cornea. Opacification or dislocation of the lens due to trauma or the development of cataracts at birth (congenital) or later in life can prevent the focusing of light. The opacified lens (i.e., a cataract) can be replaced with a new lens to restore sight. Inflammation inside the eye (endophthalmitis or uveitis) can result in white blood cell accumulation that impairs the flow of light and scars the anterior or posterior chamber of the eye. Topical antibiotics and steroids can decrease inflammation, and removal of the vitreous (vitrectomy) can restore vision.

Retinal problems include occlusion of retinal vessels, detachment of the retina, or degeneration of the macula. An occlusion of the central artery is equivalent to a stroke in the eye. Oxygen delivery to the active nerve cells of the eye becomes immediately impaired, and damage may become irreversible within several hours. Retinal vein occlusion of the eye can also deprive the eye of oxygen as blood flow and oxygen delivery through the eye's capillaries are impaired. Retinal detachment or retinal tears separate the photoreceptor cells from the retina, preventing light transmission from photocells to the optic nerve. Affected people may see sudden flashes of light or large floaters. Treatment is surgery to remove the vitreous and may require an injection of a gas bubble to hold the detached portion of the retina in place until it heals. Other retinal conditions include inflammation or bleeding due to the growth of weakened blood vessels from diseases such as diabetes. Macular degeneration is the progressive, irreversible loss of the nerve cells in the central vision, leading to blurry vision.

Neuronal pathway problems include inflammation or pressure on the optic nerve that prevents transmission of nerve signals. Intracranial masses such as pituitary tumors or brain aneurysms may cause pressure on the optic nerves or optic chiasm. Impaired blood flow through the vertebral artery of the brain that delivers oxygen to the occipital lobe may cause a stroke and loss of function in the area of the brain responsible for processing the images sent by the optic nerve.

Lessons from Healing the Blind

Healing blind people is one of the most common miracles performed by the Savior. He healed six people on four occasions. Repeated events in the scriptures should catch our attention. Although there are many lessons we can learn as we compare and contrast the accounts of the healing of the six blind men, I will highlight four principles we can learn from these four accounts.

Engage in Individualized and Customized Ministering.

We can learn how to become more like the Savior by learning *what* he did and *how* he did it. As we compare the four accounts, what is evident is how individualized and customized the Savior's ministry was. While he touched the eyes of the blind men in Matthew, and they immediately received their sight, to the blind man in Mark, he carefully led him out of the town, spat in his eyes, and healed him in phases before restoring his vision in full. To the blind man in John, he spat on the ground, formed a paste out of the dirt, rubbed it on his eyes, and then asked him to wash in the Siloam pool. Although the result of vision restoration was the same, the means and methods to get there differed. Today, we are asked to care for God's children in "higher and holier ways."[6] As we minister to one another, we are asked to do so in an individualized and customized manner. There is no longer the "one size fits all" approach or the "do unto others as ye would have them do unto you." Instead, we are asked to "do unto others as they would have us do unto them." This description of ministering and the importance of customized individuality is instructive.

> "The ways in which we can love and minister to one another are limitless. Every child of God is unique; therefore, effective ministering must be highly individualized and led by the Spirit. What works for one may not work for another."[7]

While it is not clear whether one method Jesus used to heal the blind would have only worked for one individual and not another, it appears the Savior is trying to emphasize the importance of customized ministering. Elder Stevenson, about the parable of the lost sheep and ministering to the one, taught that ministering is to be "led by the Spirit, flexible, and customized to the needs of each member."[8]

Trust in the Lord's Timing

It can be easy to get discouraged when we compare how the Lord works with us to the accounts of others we read in the scriptures. We read of the dramatic 180 turns by Alma the Younger and the sons of Mosiah, Saul, on the way to Damascus after seeing an angel, King Lamoni, and his family's conversion when being taught by Ammon, or Enos after his prayer marathon. We may wonder why similar interventions or events don't occur in our lives or with wayward family members or friends we love. Similarly, when we read of Jesus raising the dead, healing the withered hand, causing the lame to walk, or the blind to see, we may question our faith in the power of the Savior to heal when such miracles do not immediately occur in our own life. President Benson taught an important truth when applying such events to our lives.

> "But we must be cautious as we discuss these remarkable examples. Though they are real and powerful, they are the exception more than the rule. For every Paul, for every Enos, and for every King Lamoni, there are hundreds and thousands of people who find the process of repentance much more subtle, much more imperceptible."[9]

Though President Benson spoke about the dramatic process of changing our hearts and repentance through the power of the Savior's atonement, the same can be said regarding the Savior's power to heal. Though most scriptural accounts document dramatic instantaneous healing, the account in Mark of the blind man, who was brought to Jesus and was healed in stages, is a reminder that healing can be an incremental process that requires time. The first stage consisted of him going from complete blindness to seeing men "like trees walking," meaning he could now see vague objects but nothing close to reality or complete healing. Only when the Savior placed his hands upon him again and "made him look up" during the second stage of healing could he see everything clearly.

Looking up symbolizes turning to God, leaning not unto our own understanding, and trusting His ways. It implies a surrender of will, turning from not my will, but thine be done. As we seek physical, mental, emotional, or spiritual healing, we must continually look up to God as our source of power and strength. Our journey of healing may also require several stages until reaching completion, which may or may not come in this life. Elder Bednar teaches:

> "We recognize a principle that applies to every devoted disciple: strong faith in the Savior is submissively accepting of His will and timing in our

lives—even if the outcome is not what we hoped for or wanted."[10]

Adversity is not always a consequence of sin

The details in John's account of the Savior healing the blind man emphasize the prevailing, yet erroneous, thought of the time that when bad things happen, it is because the person has sinned or deserves a consequence. The first question out of the mouth of the disciples was whether the cause of this blindness was either the man's or his parent's sin. Given that multiple physical ailments had previously been cured by the Savior casting out evil spirits, it seems only natural that Jesus' disciples would assume that this man's blindness could be related to a consequence of sin. Similarly, it can be easy for us to have similar thought patterns regarding our trials and adversity. We may erroneously think that when we face hardship, adversity, or trials, we are somehow "getting what we deserve" or "aren't good enough." Although some adversity results from our own poor choices or the poor choices of others, much of life's adversity is simply a natural part of our mortal experience.[11]

As we can learn from this miracle, adversity doesn't have to lead to suffering but instead can be a means by which the "works of God should be made manifest." Adam Miller discusses this miracle in the context of a commonly misconstrued view of the purpose of suffering. He states:

> "the doctrine of original sin is an explanation for suffering...we suffer because we're being punished, we deserve to be punished because we are sinful, and we're sinful because we have inherited this sinful nature from Adam and Eve...in short "original sin is the idea that suffering is always deserved."[12]

Adam Miller asserts that God's original plan was not sin but God's original plan was grace. Although adversity can lead to suffering, through the Savior's grace, it can be repurposed for our good. He writes:

> "Does suffering, in general, have a purpose? No. Suffering is just a fact of life. But, suffering can, by way of grace, be given a purpose. In addition to being relieved, it can be redeemed. It can teach and strengthen and empower. It can, in God's Hands, be repurposed for growth and progress. God doesn't insist that [we] suffer. God's work is to relieve and redeem that suffering."[13]

This doctrine that God wants to relieve our suffering is clearly outlined in Doctrine and Covenants 19:16. "For behold, I, God, have suffered these things for all, that they might not suffer if they would repent." We often equate repentance as something we do to alleviate the negative consequences of sin. However, President Nelson taught that repentance is much more than this.

> "The word for repentance in the Greek New Testament is metanoeo. The prefix meta- means "change." The suffix -noeo is related to Greek words that mean "mind," "knowledge," "spirit," and "breath." Thus, when Jesus asks you and me to "repent," He is inviting us to change our mind, our knowledge, our spirit—even the way we breathe. He is asking us to change the way we love, think, serve, spend our time, treat our wives, teach our children, and even care for our bodies."[14]

Repentance must also include changing the way we view adversity, trials, and tribulations. By doing so, through the grace of the Savior Jesus Christ, God can help relieve our suffering as we ask him to view our trials through a new lens. Perhaps this is why the Savior replied to the prophet Joseph

Smith's prayer as he pleaded for God to remember the suffering of the saints, saying,

> "Peace be unto thy soul; thine adversity and thine afflictions shall be but a small moment; And then, if thou endure it well, God shall exalt thee on high... know thou, my son, that all these things shall give the experience, and shall be for thy good."[15]

As we face life's challenges, adversity, and trials, repentance means to place our trust in the Savior more fervently and take his yoke upon us through making and keeping covenants. Through His grace, we need not continue to suffer but can be exalted to a higher level of spiritual development, and our trials can be turned for our good.

Our Ways are not the Lord's Ways

If you have ever scratched your eye (corneal abrasion), or had sand or dirt get into your eye, you know just how painful it can be. Blinking hurts, and attempting to open or move your eyes elicits more pain and tears. I experienced an extreme version of this when I underwent a corrective eye surgery known as PRK. My cornea's surface was shaped so that I couldn't see very well at far distances, and one of my eyes had an irregular surface known as an astigmatism. This meant I was not a good candidate for LASIK correction. Lasik is a relatively quick and painless operation where a small flap is made on the surface of the cornea, and the flap is then folded back. A laser reshapes the inner cornea, and the flap is placed back over the eye's surface. Instead, PRK uses a laser to essentially burn off and reshape the entire visual cornea, and then, over time, the skin cells regrow over the surface of the reshaped cornea. With topical anesthetic in my eye, the machine focused and shot several lasers, reshaping both of my corneas. The laser machine moved away, and as drops were placed in my eye, for a moment, the previously blurry words that were taped on the ceiling of the surgery center came into clear focus: "Believe in Miracles." The bliss of the moment, however, was replaced a few hours later by excruciating pain as the numbing drops wore off. As I lay in a dark room, with cold compresses on my eye, applying drops every hour, I regretted my decision. This pain process continued for the next several days. However, fast forward to now, seeing at distances without glasses or contacts has indeed been a miracle.

As anesthesiologists, we do our best to protect the eyes of our patients from getting inadvertently injured.[16] When this occasionally occurs despite our best preventative efforts, the pain patients experience can be more painful than recovering from the surgery itself. Knowing how painful scratched eyes can be, it can seem totally illogical that the Savior would spit in the dirt and rub the paste in the eyes of the two blind men healed in Mark and John.

However, as stated in Isaiah, the Lord reminds us that "my thoughts are not your thoughts, neither are your ways my ways."[17] It seemed illogical for the widow of Zarephath to take the last of her oil and cornmeal and make a cake first for the prophet Elijah when she and her son were about to die. However, by her demonstration of faith, the blessings of the Lord rained down upon her, and she and her household could eat for many days.[18] It may not make sense to pay your tithing when you first receive your paycheck when your budget calculations indicate you will not have enough to cover your monthly needs. However, by paying with faith, Elder Bednar testifies that "we often receive significant but subtle blessings that are not always what we expect and easily can be overlooked."[19] He teaches some of these subtle blessings may include increased patience, physical or mental stamina, the ability to constrain our desires, a greater capacity to act and change our circumstances, or "increased temporal and spiritual capacity to do more with less, a keener ability to prioritize and simplify, and an enhanced ability to take proper care of the material possessions we already have acquired."[20] It may not have seemed logical for the widow with two mites to cast in her all instead of just her abundance, but that is what the Savior specifically taught is necessary.[21]

Reflection
1. How have I seen the Lord individualize his healing approach to my life?
2. How has experiencing trials, hardships, or adversity helped me deepen my testimony or strengthen my faith in Jesus?
3. How can I customize and individualize my acts of kindness, compassion, and service to those around me?

---

[1] "For the Beauty of the Earth," Hymn 98

[2] Alma 30:44

[3] Matthew 13:14-16

[4] C.S. Lewis, "They Asked For A Paper," in Is Theology Poetry? (London: Geoffrey Bless, 1962), 165

[5] D&C 88:13

[6] Russell M. Nelson. "Closing Remarks," General Conference, Oct 2019

[7] ministering.churchofjesuschrist.org

[8] Gary E. Stevenson. "Shepherding Souls," General Conference, October 2018

[9] Ezra Taft Benson. "Might Change of Heart," Ensign, Oct 1989

[10] David A Bednar. "Accepting the Lord's Will and Timing," Ensign, August 2016

[11] Come Follow Me - YW. "Why do we have adversity?" https://www.churchofjesuschrist.org/study/youth/learn/yw/plan-of-salvation/adversity?lang=eng

[12] Adam Miller. Original Grace, page 12

[13] Miller, Adam. Original Grace, page 34

[14] Russell M. Nelson. "We Can Do Better and Be Better," General Conference, April 2019

[15] D&C 121:6-8, and 122:7

[16] sometimes, under general anesthesia, a patient's eyes do not completely close and can dry out and become painful. When coming out of anesthesia, patients may inadvertently rub their eyes and scratch the surface, causing a corneal abrasion.

[17] Isaiah 55:8

[18] 1 Kings 17:9-15

[19] David A. Bednar, "Windows of Heaven," General Conference, Oct 2013

[20] David A. Bednar, "Windows of Heaven," General Conference, Oct 2013

[21] Luke 21:1-4

Chapter 11

Jesus Heals a Withered Hand

Despite multiple attempts to do so, it became nearly impossible for the Pharisees to explain away the miracles Jesus was performing for countless people. Jesus was "healing all manner of sickness and all manner of disease among the people. And his fame went throughout all Syria."[1] Those who were healed were growing, and those who witnessed his healing were increasing exponentially. When Jesus healed a blind man, the Pharisees attempted to prove the man was an imposter and wasn't blind since birth. When Jesus cast out evil spirits, they called Jesus the prince of devils and claimed that he was using demonic power. However, their attempts were no match for the Son of God. Although the Pharisees began to accuse Jesus of violating established Mosaic laws like the Law of the Sabbath, in rebuttal, Jesus asserts that He is the Lord of the Sabbath. To emphasize this point, Jesus entered the synagogue on the Sabbath to find a man with a withered hand. After teaching that it is lawful to do well on the sabbath day, He asked the man to stretch forth his withered hand, and Jesus heals him.

In Matthew 12:10-13 we read:
> 10 And, behold, there was a man which had his hand withered. And they asked him, saying, Is it lawful to heal on the sabbath days? that they might accuse him.
> 11 And he said unto them, What man shall there be among you, that shall have one sheep, and if it fall into a pit on the sabbath day, will he not lay hold on it, and lift it out?
> 12 How much then is a man better than a sheep? Wherefore it is lawful to do well on the sabbath days.

13 Then saith he to the man, Stretch forth thine hand. And he stretched it forth; and it was restored whole, like as the other.

The Miracle of Our Hands

The human hand contains 27 bones and is divided into three sections. Eight carpal bones comprise the wrist, five metacarpal bones compose the middle part of the hand, and 14 bones make up the phalanges (fingers). Numerous ligaments, tendons, sheaths, arteries, veins, nerves, and muscles exist within the hand. Although a few interosseous muscles in the hand's metacarpal section allow the fingers to spread apart, most of the muscles that control the movement of the fingers and wrist are located in the forearm. On the palm side of the hand, three interosseous muscles pull our fingers together, and on the back side, four interosseous muscles spread our fingers apart. There are dedicated muscles that move our 5th finger and thumb. Three hypothenar muscles - the abductor, flexor, and opponens digiti minimi - allow the pinky to move away from the ring finger, bend at the joint, or move toward the thumb, respectively. Three thenar muscles - the abductor, flexor, and opponens pollicis - perform the same functions for the thumb. Lumbrical muscles allow the fingers to straighten.

Each forearm muscle connects to tendons that travel through a tendon sheath called the flexor retinaculum on the palm or the extensor retinaculum on the back. These muscles allow the fingers to flex or extend. Three flexor muscles - flexor pollicis longus, digitorum profundus, digitorum superficialis - flex the thumb, the tips of the other four fingers, or the middle joint of our four fingers, respectively. The flexor carpi ulnaris deviates the wrist away from the thumb, while the flexor carpi radialis and palmaris longus muscle bend the wrist. Notably, the palmaris longus is often absent in nearly 25% of people, but when present, it can be used to rebuild injured tendons, given it is not essential. On the extensor side

- the extension pollicis longus extends the thumb, and the extensor digitorum communis allows for the extension of each of the four fingers. The extensor carpi ulnaris straightens and stabilizes the wrist and can help move the wrist away from the thumb, while the extensor carpi radialis longus straightens and stabilizes and pulls the wrist in toward the thumb side. Additionally, pronator and supinator muscles in the proximal forearm assist in rotating the hand palm side up (supination) or palm side down (pronation).

Two major arteries supply blood to the hand: the radial and ulnar arteries. They originate from the axillary artery, a major artery that comes off of the aorta initially as the subclavian artery. When these two arteries reach the hand, they split into superficial and deep palmar branches and then arch back around and connect to form a superficial and deep palmar arch. The arches give off common digital arteries that travel toward the fingers and then split again near the web spaces of the fingers to become proper digital arteries. Each proper digital artery supplies blood to two different fingers. The redundant arterial connections of the hand help maintain oxygen delivery to the fingers in the event of an injury.

Three main nerves supply sensation and motor function to the hand: the median, radial, and ulnar nerves. The nerves originate from the cervical trunks coming off the spinal cord of the neck from C5-T1. The ulnar nerve runs close to your elbow and is the "funny bone" nerve. It powers the muscles of the forearm that flex the wrist and fingers, the thenar and hypothenar muscles that close the hand and allow the thumb and finger to touch and provides sensation to the palmar surface of the pinky and ring finger. Injury to this nerve can lead to clawing of the ring and pinky finger and the inability to spread apart the fingers. The radial nerve travels along the humerus bone and is susceptible to injury when the humerus is broken. It then travels along the forearm, powers the extensor muscles of the hand and wrist along, and provides sensation to the thumb and back of the hand. The median nerve controls the flexor muscles of the wrist along with the pointer and middle finger. It supplies sensation to the palm side of the hand, thumb, index, middle, and half of the ringer finger. Because it crosses the wrist, it can be compressed at this location, causing pain and weakness called carpal tunnel syndrome.

The anatomical detail provided is not intended to make the reader an expert in the anatomy of the hand. Instead, it should engender a deep appreciation for the miracle of our hands and fingers. In each finger, over 3,000 touch receptors respond to pressure changes, and our entire hand has as many touch receptors as the whole skin on our abdomen or back. These touch receptors allow our fingers to distinguish between points that are less than 1 mm apart and can do so quickly and accurately. In fact, although one can visually read at a speed of 300 words a minute, a person using braille can read as much as 400 words a minute using both hands. Our hands are indeed a miracle!

A Withered Hand

Similar to diseases of the central nervous system, disruption anywhere on the peripheral nerve pathway can cause signs and symptoms of disease. Pain, numbness, weakness, and even muscle atrophy may occur when nerves are injured. Narrowed foramen of the cervical bones in the neck may entrap the nerve roots of C5-T1 and cause pain, weakness, or numbness in the arm or hand on the same side. The brachial plexus, the precursor to the individual nerves of the arm and hand, travels between the clavicle and the first rib and can become trapped when lifting one's arm, leading to symptoms of pain or weakness called thoracic outlet syndrome. The ulnar nerve travels along the ulnar groove of the elbow, and cubital tunnel syndrome results when compressed. A compressed median nerve results in carpal tunnel syndrome. The radial nerve can be stretched or damaged when the humerus bone is injured or from prolonged direct compression of the radial nerve on the upper arm. Injuries can also occur from entrapment in the forearm.

In these mononeuropathies (single nerve injury), weakness and eventual atrophy of muscles can result in persistent hand deformities. When the ulnar nerve is injured, a claw hand formation results and one cannot extend the fingers at the interphalangeal joints, resulting in permanent flexion. In an injury of the median nerve, known as the "hand of benediction" or "preacher's hand," the pointer finger cannot flex, while an intact ulnar nerve allows the pinky and ring finger to flex. With a radial nerve injury, there is a complete wrist drop, and the fingers cannot extend. Some scholars believe the man with the withered hand had a radial palsy because being asked to stretch forth his hand as an act of healing would suggest it was flexed, and the wrist and fingers would appear withered like a withered flower that bends inward to the stem. Additionally, several works of art detailing this miracle between the 10th and 16th centuries depict a radial nerve palsy. Scholars postulate that either this represented the passing down through generations a detailed description by people familiar with the miracle or, more likely, that they knew actual people who suffered from this condition. For example, a condition known as saturnine palsy can cause radial nerve palsy due to lead poisoning. This affected the general population, especially artists who worked with leaded paints.

Whether the man with the withered hand suffered from a mononeuropathy like radial nerve palsy or not, acute injuries can take several months or even years to heal. A peripheral nerve is composed of thousands of individual fibers, much like a twine rope, which is made up of thousands of individual small fiber strands. If one of those small strands is stretched, crushed, cut, or injured, the action of the particular nerve - motor (causing a muscle to contract) or sensory (carrying touch, pain, temperature) - no longer works.

The extent of injury may determine the time required to recover. In the mildest form of injury, neuropraxia, the nerve axon fiber is still intact. Still, an area of demyelination (disruption of the insulating sheath around nerves that exists to prevent signal and conduction loss) causes temporary loss of function. Neuropraxia may take anywhere from a few weeks to a few months to recover. However, if the injury damages the axon, the nerve will degenerate back to the cell body of the nerve located near the spinal cord in a process called Wallerian degeneration. If the nerve scaffolding is still intact, the nerve may regenerate from the level of the spinal cord to the effect site at about 1-3 mm a day until function is restored. If the nerve scaffolding is damaged, such as through transection, and the nerve scaffolding ends are near one another, the nerve will attempt to regenerate. Still, the likelihood of reconnection decreases, and the probability that the deficit may be permanent increases. Sometimes, the severed peripheral nerve can be identified and sewn back together. If the distance is too great, the nerve ends can be sewn to a conduit that helps guide the regenerating nerve as it grows to reestablish nerve connections. Similarly, a nerve graft can be sewn between the two ends to restore some function. Finally, if muscles are atrophied or nerves are permanently damaged, the arm has been blessed with muscles that frequently have dual functions. Hand surgeons can transfer a tendon or part of a tendon of one muscle to another joint in the hand to restore function.

The Savior, the master physician and creator of our hands, intimately understands every intricate detail. Given this man's hand was withered, it suggests this process has been going on for a long period with a seemingly irreversible condition. Muscles may have atrophied and turned into scar tissue. Tendons that have not been extended for some time may be permanently shortened. Joints that haven't moved may be permanently locked in place. But if faith in Jesus Christ can move mountains, certainly it could move one's hand again.

The Hand of Faith

Significantly, Jesus Christ didn't reflexively speak or touch the man's hand to heal him. Instead, the Savior first commanded the man to "stretch forth thine hand."[2] It was only AFTER the man stretched forth his hand, something he perhaps had been unable to do for a long time, that his hand was "restored whole, like the other."[3] Orson Pratt explained:

> "When the man with the withered hand was healed, the Lord did not say I command you to be healed, without any act on his part; but he commanded him to stretch forth his hand. That, apparently, was an impossibility, for his arm was withered, powerless; and he might have thought that it was impossible for him to perform the act required of him. But an exercise of faith was required on the part of that man—something connected with the mental faculties, by which the blessing of healing might be secured."[4]

The miracle of the withered hand emphasizes the gospel principle that faith precedes the miracle. In the bible dictionary, we learn that "faith is a principle of action and power" and that faith is "more than belief, since true faith always moves its possessor to some kind of physical and mental action." Although it may have been years since the man could stretch forth his hand, he followed what Jesus asked him to do. It started with a desire, became a hope, and then a mental action in his mind that told his hand to move. This faith was sufficient to move him from just a thought to the physical act of stretching out his hand. This demonstration of faith was requisite AND sufficient for the Savior to heal him.

Moroni teaches that:

> 16. Yea, and even all they who wrought miracles wrought them by faith, even those who were before Christ and also those who were after.

18. And neither at any time hath any wrought miracles **until after their faith**; wherefore they first believed in the Son of God.[5]

How can we demonstrate sufficient faith to experience miracles in our own lives? Mark L. Pace, Sunday School General President at the time, suggests five patterns of faith that we should make part of our day-to-day lives:

1. Following the Lord's living prophet
2. Attending our Sunday meetings
3. Participating in home-centered gospel learning
4. Paying tithes and offerings
5. Attending the temple

He further teaches that when we do so, "[we] demonstrate [our] faith in Jesus Christ and qualify for the miracles that God has prepared."[6] Just as the man with the withered hand was asked to demonstrate his faith before receiving a miracle, we must demonstrate our faith in Jesus for Him to work miracles in our lives.

Reflection
1. What areas of discipleship can I more fully extend my hand toward to qualify for the miracles God has prepared for me?
2. Identify faith barriers that prevent you from moving from desire to mental action to physical action. How can you eliminate these barriers?
3. Record in your own life when faith has preceded the miracle.

---

[1] Matt 4:23-24

[2] Matthew 12:13

[3] Matthew 12:13

[4] Orson Pratt, Journal of Discourses 14:292a

[5] Ether 12:16,18 (Emphasis Added)

[6] Mark L. Pace. "Faith Still Proceeds the Miracle," BYU Speeches, Oct 29, 2019

Chapter 12

Jesus Heals the Hearing and Speech Impaired Man

In his travels between the Mediterranean Sea (town of Tyre) and the Sea of Galilee (coast of Decapolis), Jesus had a man brought to him who had two disabilities - he was unable to hear and unable to speak. The multitude desired for Jesus to touch the man and heal him. He put his fingers in his ears and then, after spitting, touched his tongue. His hearing was restored, and his speech was now plain to understand. Mark describes everyone as "beyond measure astonished, saying, He hath done all things well."[1]

The following account of the miracle described in the book of Mark chapter 7 is as follows:

> 31 And again, departing from the coasts of Tyre and Sidon, he came unto the sea of Galilee, through the midst of the coasts of Decapolis.
> 32 And they bring unto him one that was deaf, and had an impediment in his speech; and they beseech him to put his hand upon him.
> 33 And he took him aside from the multitude, and put his fingers into his ears, and he spit, and touched his tongue;
> 34 And looking up to heaven, he sighed, and saith unto him, Ephphatha, that is, Be opened.
> 35 And straightway his ears were opened, and the string of his tongue was loosed, and he spake plain.
> 36 And he charged them that they should tell no man: but the more he charged them, so much the more a great deal they published it;
> 37 And were beyond measure astonished, saying, He hath done all things well: he maketh both the deaf to hear, and the dumb to speak.

The Miracle of Hearing

Hearing is receiving sound waves and converting them into nerve impulses that the brain can interpret and attach to familiar and previously associated sounds. The process of hearing can be broken down into four anatomical parts: the outer, middle, and inner ear, and the neuronal. The outer ear includes the ear, formally known as the pinna, attached to the head, and the external auditory canal to the tympanic membrane, or ear drum. The designed purpose of the external ear is to capture sound waves that travel toward a person and focus them down the canal to convert sound waves into mechanical waves as they strike the tympanic membrane.

When sound waves strike the tympanic membrane, it causes three small bones in the middle ear, the malleus, incas, and stapes, to move. They are often compared to a hammer, anvil, and stirrup because of their shape and function. The stapes bone is attached to a membrane known as the oval window, separating the air-filled middle ear from the fluid-filled inner ear. The vibration of the stapes against the oval window converts the mechanical motion of the middle ear bones back into fluid pressure waves that travel through the inner ear's fluid within the cochlea.

Hair cells attached to the cochlea's surface move in response to the fluid waves, much like plants attached to the bottom of the ocean floor, which move back and forth with ocean waves. These hair cells come in different sizes and, consequently, bend depending on the different frequencies of waves generated by the vibration on the oval window. When a hair cell is sufficiently bent, sodium ion channels open up, and sodium ions flow inside the hair cells. This flow of ions results in a nerve action potential that releases neurotransmitter chemicals that activate the auditory nerve. This entire process converts sound waves into mechanical waves, fluid waves, and nerve impulses that travel along the auditory nerve to the primary auditory cortex of the brain's temporal lobe.

There are two inner ear muscles - the tensor tympani and the stapedius muscles. The tensor tympani attaches to the malleus and serves as a shock absorber to dampen loud noises. Although the reaction time isn't quick enough to react to sudden loud noises such as a gunshot or an explosion, the muscle can dampen sounds like shouting, thunder, or chewing. Similar to the shocks on the fork of a bicycle or car, when loud noises bounce off the tympanic membrane, which would then cause the malleus to move greater distances, the tensor tympani muscle tightens to decrease the length of displacement. This reduces the distance the malleus moves, which decreases the movement of the stapes on the oval window, resulting in a dampening of the fluid wave through the cochlea compared to the initial air sound wave. The stapedius muscle, the shortest muscle in the body at only 6 mm in length, attaches to the stapes bone and further attenuates loud sound waves over 85 decibels to decrease the fluid wave transmissions in the inner ear.

Not only can the muscles and bones of the ear serve to dampen loud noises, but they can also amplify quiet sounds in two ways. First, the difference in size between the malleus and the smaller stapes bone allows the sound pressure it receives from the tympanic membrane (55 square millimeters surface area) to be applied to a smaller oval window (3.2 square millimeters surface area). Thus, the energy of the sound waves hitting the tympanic membrane concentrates on a smaller area and, therefore, can apply more energy to the inner ear. Second, because the malleus is larger, it moves a greater distance and thus applies more energy on the incus that connects to the stapes. The result of the two amplification techniques means that when no dampening via the middle ear muscles occurs, the force applied to the oval window is about 22 times greater than the force of the sound waves applied to the tympanic membrane. This allows the ears to comprehend even the faintest whisper. In short, the bones and muscles of the middle ear work together to amplify quiet sounds to improve hearing perception and dampen loud noises to protect the system from damage. Hearing is a miracle!

The Miracle of Speech

When sound enters the temporal lobe in the form of language, it is recognized in an area of the brain known as Wernicke's area. This area receives input from the primary auditory cortex and assigns meaning and context. People with damage to this area of the brain often cannot process spoken words. Furthermore, they cannot form coherent phrases when they attempt to speak. They often uninterruptedly speak words together that have no meaning, resulting in a sort of "word salad." The creation of speech occurs in an entirely different part of the brain known as Broca's area. People who have damage to Broca's area have expressive aphasia - they can think what they want to say but are unable to form words to say it. Although there can be a large spectrum of symptoms, in general, many can comprehend speech but have word-finding and word-fluency difficulties. Unlike people with damage to Wernicke's area who are unaware of their incoherency, people with expressive aphasia recognize their disability and, therefore, are incredibly frustrated while trying to speak.

Speaking is one of the more complicated tasks we perform as humans. In a simple analogy, it can be compared to the building of a house. The first stage of speech formation includes neuronal pathways involved in conceptual planning (ideas, thoughts, feelings, and words that circulate our brain's consciousness only known to us). The planning stage often involves our entire brain as it draws on past memories, emotions, and feelings stored in many different areas. This is analogous to a pre-houseplan drawing stage where you consider what type of house you would like and ask yourself questions such as "How big?" "How do you want to feel in your house?" How do you want the house traffic to flow?" Or "What are your goals for the house?" Next, these concepts must be directed toward linguistic and motor planning. Linguistic planning involves drawing upon prepackaged phonemes (sounds) and organizing them into word and sentence structures. This planning is still in the premotor stages but most often concentrates in the dominant hemisphere of the person, which is usually the left hemisphere for right-handed people. This speaking stage may be analogous to reviewing conceptual drawings of your home, basic floor plans and level plans, and basic exterior designs and features. Once these linguistic roadmaps are created, motor planning begins. Much like an architect takes desired concepts to draw detailed blueprints, Broca's area begins to string together the motor commands for each phoneme and plans pitch, intensity of sound, and timing.

These phonetic blueprint plans are transmitted to the basal ganglia and cerebellum, the motor circuits executing the blueprints. The basal ganglia serve to fine-tune muscle tone and contraction. It is likened to a finish carpenter that puts the final touches on the executed blueprints to smooth out irregularities and imperfections. It dampens and refines the movement signals received from the motor cortex. The cerebellum receives a copy of the executed plans and compares them to the sensory feedback mechanisms it receives when the plans for speech are executed. Consider it the general contractor that checks the work of the builders to verify that architect plans are being executed as intended. The cerebellum receives feedback called proprioception (nerves that send information to the brain regarding where the muscles are in space, how they are contracting, and how they are responding to the commands they receive) and makes course corrections in real-time. It may take the sound that the auditory nerve initially receives and realize that it is too loud in its creation when a whisper was intended and signal back to the basal ganglia to decrease the sound intensity by adjusting the muscles based on how they are contracting. It is similar to the homeowner who is on-site when the building is underway and may stop the process and request real-time changes or adjustments.

The nerve tract responsible for speech is called the corticobulbar tract. It is the nerve pathway that executes the functions received from the cerebellum through the motor and nerves of the cranial nerves. Of the twelve cranial nerves, one assists in speech modulation through the hearing system via the vestibulocochlear nerve, and five others control the 45 muscles directly involved in speech production and modulation. Speech truly is a miracle!

Ears to Hear

As the guide to the scriptures teaches, references to ears are "often used as a symbol of a person's ability to hear and understand the things of God."[2] Consider how King Benjamin opened his famous sermon by saying, "hearken unto me, and open your ears that ye may hear, and your hearts that ye may understand, and your minds that the mysteries of God may be unfolded to your view."[3] Amulek admits, "I was called many times and I would not hear."[4] When asked by the Savior's disciples why he spoke in parables, the Savior explained that people's "ears are dull of hearing" and therefore "by hearing ye shall hear, and shall not understand."[5] However, in the context of the restored gospel, Jesus teaches that the voice of the Lord is for everyone and that no ear shall not hear his voice.[6] The key is to humble oneself through prayer so that "[our] ears can be open that [we] may hear."[7]

It is important to note that although we are commanded to be in the world but not of the world, we are spiritual beings meant to have earthly experiences and not mortal beings trying to have spiritual experiences. Because of the veil, we largely don't remember our premortal life with our physical brains. However, our spirits remember, and heaven tries to communicate with us.

The prophet Elijah had an experience with how the Lord communicates to us. Before this experience, the prophet Elijah had just taken on the wicked prophets of Baal. To prove who the real God of Israel is compared to the false Gods of Baal, he challenged them to try and call down from heaven fire to consume the offered sacrifice. It was one Elijah versus four hundred fifty "prophets" of Baal. After failed attempts by the prophets of Baal, Elijah instructed them to douse Elijah's altar with water three times. Despite being soaked to the core and filled with water, the Lord consumed the offering and evaporated all the water. All the false prophets were slain by a sword, and a great rain came. However, Elijah soon found himself depressed under a Juniper tree, hoping to die.[8] An angel restored his strength. He was able to travel to the Mount of Horeb, where he was instructed to stand upon the mount before the Lord.[9] It was there he experienced the still small voice.

> 11 And, behold, the Lord passed by, and a great and strong wind rent the mountains, and brake in pieces the rocks before the Lord; but the Lord was not in the wind: and after the wind an earthquake; but the Lord was not in the earthquake:
> 12 And after the earthquake a fire; but the Lord was not in the fire: and after the fire a still small voice.
> 13 And it was so...

Although feeling completely abandoned and alone, Elijah could communicate with the Lord through the still, small voice. He received the direction to anoint kings over Syria and Israel and prophets to support him in his ministry.

The function of our ears to amplify or dampen sound waves that come our way can be instructive as we consider how we can receive communication from God through the medium of the still, small voice of the Holy Ghost to our spirits. The sound of the world can be constant, loud, and overpowering. We must strengthen our spiritual tensor tympani and stapedius muscles to dampen the world's effects on our abilities to hear the still, small voice of the spirit. Just like our hearing system has a built-in design to amplify quiet noises, we are designed to hear the still, small voice of the Holy Ghost through the light of Christ, which is in every individual.

However, many things would attempt to derail our ability to hear and understand spiritual things. President Nelson taught,

> "If most of the information you get comes from social or other media, your ability to hear the whisperings of the Spirit will be diminished. If you are not also seeking the Lord through daily prayer and gospel study, you leave yourself vulnerable to philosophies that may be intriguing but are not true. Even Saints who are otherwise faithful can be derailed by the steady beat of Babylon's band."[10]

He further urges us to make time for the Lord every day. Doing so strengthens our spiritual stapedius muscle and appropriately tightens our tensor tympani. We can also use the shock-absorbing function of these muscles to lessen the effects of the loud and deceptive false happiness the world attempts to peddle to us by instead taking time each day to pray and ponder. We have been urged to develop our own sacred groves where we can retreat, connect with heaven, and ask the questions of our hearts.[11] We have been asked by Jesus Christ himself to pray secretly in our own closets so we can be rewarded openly.[12] Furthermore, the prophet has urged us to make time for the Lord in his Holy house through temple service and worship. President Nelson promises that "increased time in the temple will bless your life in ways nothing else can" and then urges us to "focus on the temple in ways you never have before."[13]

The more we feel the Holy Ghost, the more we will feel the Holy Ghost. Yes, this is written correctly. It becomes a positive feedback loop. When we recognize and feel the Holy Ghost it means we have received the Holy Ghost. And when we receive the Holy Ghost, we are sanctified by the Holy Ghost.[14] The more sanctified we become, the better we can receive the Holy Ghost, and the better we are at recognizing him when he communicates. Just like our natural ears receive sound input all the time, our brains are good at ignoring sound waves even after they are converted to electrical impulses that travel along the cochlear nerve. How often have you been focused on a book or a television show, or have you been deep in thought when someone has had to repeat your name or a question several times before it registers they are trying to talk to you? Similarly, just because we may not recognize or register experiences with heaven through the Holy Ghost, it doesn't mean God isn't trying to communicate with us.

For a variety of reasons, we are not able to hear. Just because we have received the gift of the Holy Ghost doesn't mean we have the power of the Holy Ghost. Increased power comes through increased righteous living. The more virtuous we live, the easier spiritual promptings will flow into our minds and hearts. The flow of electricity can be expressed in the formula $I=V/R$. Flow (I) is equal to the voltage potential (V) divided by the resistance (R). Because God is infinite in voltage compared to us, we could theoretically receive an infinite flow of guidance, inspiration, comfort, and love from heaven. The only limit is our resistance. The smaller the size of a wire, the greater the resistance and, therefore, the more limited the flow of power through that wire. A larger wire has less resistance and, therefore, a greater flow of power. When we consistently exercise our agency to become true disciples of Jesus Christ at all times and in all places, "line upon line, precept upon precept, here a little and there a little," we add more conductive copper to our wire that connects our spirits to heaven. This decreased resistance increases the flow of spiritual power through the Holy Ghost in our lives. We will experience the fruits of the Spirit more abundantly.[15] We will have more peace. Like Elijah, we will find the Lord in the still, small voice.

Reflection:
1. Create your own sacred grove - a place in your home, car, or nature where you can consistently retreat to this place to pray and ponder the scriptures. After some time of doing this, reflect on how you feel.
2. What changes can you make to make more time for the Lord?
3. Consider times in your life when you felt close to God or when you frequently felt the Holy Ghost. What changes can you make to feel the power of the Holy Ghost more often?

---

[1] Mark 7:37

[2] Guide to the Scriptures. Topic, "Ears"

[3] Mosiah 2:9

[4] Alma 10:13

[5] Matt 13:14-15

[6] D&C 1:2

[7] D&C 136:32

[8] 1 Kings 19:4

[9] 1 Kings 19:11

[10] Russell M. Nelson. "Make Time for the Lord," General Conference, October 2021

[11] Thomas S Monson, "Choose You This Day," General Conference, October 2004.

[12] Matthew 6:6

[13] President Nelson. "Overcome the World and Find Rest," General Conference, October 2022

[14] 3 Nephi 27:20

[15] Galatians 5:22-23

Chapter 13

Jesus Heals the Man with Dropsy

Jesus frequently taught the importance of going about doing good on the Sabbath. He taught He was the Lord of the Sabbath and took opportunities to teach and do good on the Sabbath in the presence of the Pharisees on seven occasions. The last occurrence of such was when Jesus healed the man with dropsy. Given his prior healings on the Sabbath, the Savior was under particular watch and scrutiny from his accusers on that holy day. When he went to the chief of the Pharisees, there was a man with dropsy or abnormal body swelling. Knowing they were watching what he would do, he asked them whether it was against the law to heal on the Sabbath. They were silent, and the Savior took the man and healed him. Here is the following account from Luke, chapter 14.

> **1** And it came to pass, as he went into the house of one of the chief Pharisees to eat bread on the sabbath day, that they watched him.
> **2** And, behold, there was a certain man before him which had the dropsy.
> **3** And Jesus answering spake unto the lawyers and Pharisees, saying, Is it lawful to heal on the sabbath day?
> **4** And they held their peace. And he took him, and healed him, and let him go;

The Miracle of our Circulatory System

It happens 70 times a minute, 100,800 times a day, and 36.7 million times a year. It is the beat of a human heart. And if you live to be 80 years old, chances are that this heartbeat will have occurred nearly 3 billion times! If every heartbeat represents the distance of a foot, our heartbeats will travel around the world 22 times in an 80-year lifetime. And all of this happens automatically, without any mental or physical effort on our part.

The main purpose of our heart is to circulate blood around our bodies. It has two chambers that receive blood from the lungs (left atrium) or the body (right atrium) and then two chambers that pump the blood through the lungs (right ventricle) or the body (left ventricle). Blood contains about 45% red blood cells, 1% platelets, and white blood cells; the remaining 54% is called plasma. Although 90% of plasma is water, the remaining 10% contains fats, lipids, proteins, hormones, and other elements necessary for life. The primary purpose of red blood cells is to deliver oxygen to the body and remove carbon dioxide from the body. Oxygen and carbon dioxide bind to the iron portion of the red blood cell (the heme in hemoglobin). Oxygen delivery allows our cells to participate in aerobic metabolism. After delivering oxygen to our cells, hemoglobin picks up the byproduct of cellular metabolism, carbon dioxide, and carries it back to our lungs, where it is exhaled. Insufficient oxygen delivery to our cells, tissues, and organs can cause permanent injury and cell death.

Oxygen is a critical molecule our body uses to make the molecule ATP (adenosine triphosphate). It is usable energy for cellular functions. ATP to our cells is like money in our pockets. Cash allows us to purchase things that enable us to live - food, water, housing, clothing - and to have fun. Similarly, ATP allows cells to make hormones, proteins, and other molecules required to live. How would you feel if you expected to make $36/hr but were told you would only receive $2/hr for your next paycheck? Without sufficient oxygen, our cells can only generate 2 ATP instead of 36 ATP per glucose molecule to perform cellular functions. Furthermore, without adequate hemoglobin to carry oxygen and a sufficiently strong heart to circulate the hemoglobin through our body, our body's ATP energy supply for essential functions quickly disappears.

The circulatory system's additional function is to carry the necessary nutrients our bodies absorb from the digestion of food - fats, sugars, proteins, vitamins, etc - and deliver them to our cells. A complex network of veins from the stomach and small and large intestines transport these absorbed nutrients to the liver. The liver is a unique organ; most blood flow to the liver is venous and not arterial. About 75% of the blood flow to the liver comes from the portal vein, whereas only 25% comes from the hepatic artery. The liver receives approximately 25% of the blood circulating through the body and performs hundreds of critical functions. It stores vitamins required for cellular function. It creates and breaks down glycogen, the storage form of glucose. The liver produces cholesterol needed for hormones, clotting factors, and immune molecules and is an integral part of the immune system. Finally, it breaks down fats and inactivates and neutralizes countless drugs, toxins, and hormones to prepare them to be eliminated by the kidneys.

Our circulatory system also sends blood to our kidneys. Our two kidneys filter over 200 liters of blood a day. In perspective, the volume of one hundred 2 L bottles flows through our kidneys daily, and our kidneys filter 36,500 L yearly! For every 200 L of fluid that passes through our kidneys, about 1-1.5 liters of urine are produced daily. This amount is enough to fill 225 two-liter soda bottles annually! Kidneys are sensitive to changes in circulation and, therefore, play an essential role in regulating your blood pressure to ensure adequate blood delivery and filtration. Additionally, they make a hormone called erythropoietin, which stimulates red blood cell production to maintain oxygen delivery. They help control the blood's pH level, preventing your blood from being too acidic or basic, and produce a hormone that regulates calcium and phosphorus levels critical to bone health.

Dropsy

Although dropsy is an antiquated term, it means the abnormal swelling of the body. This can occur when the heart doesn't pump sufficiently (congestive heart failure), causing fluid to build up in the circulatory system, spilling over into the soft tissues, known as edema. Additionally, fluid may get backed up in and around the lungs (pleural effusion). Dropsy may have also been a consequence of inadequate blood flow through the liver. Given that 25% of the total cardiac output flows through the liver, if the liver becomes inflamed secondary to increased fat storage (steatohepatitis), toxins like alcohol (alcoholic hepatitis), or other inflammatory diseases that cause scar tissue to replace normal liver tissue, the result will be a decrease in blood flow through the liver leading to ascites (build-up of fluid in the abdominal cavity). Furthermore, as liver production of essential proteins such as albumin decreases, the circulatory system cannot retain fluid in the vessels, and water accumulates in the body outside of the circulation. Dropsy may have also occurred due to impaired kidney function. If the kidneys cannot properly eliminate extra water, it will build up in the circulation and eventually stretch the heart's muscle fibers, causing the heart to fail. Decreased heart function can further impair kidney function. This reduced blood filtration will cause the buildup of extra fluid and toxins in the body, resulting in abnormal swelling.

Our bodies contain about 60% water, most in the interstitium (space between each cell). Dozens of liters of extra fluid may accumulate outside of the circulatory system over time. Thirty-eight liters of excess fluid has been reportedly removed from a patient's abdomen (abdominal ascites). When fluid is removed from the outside of a lung (pleural effusion) through a thoracentesis procedure, the lung re-expansion can act like a sponge to soak up circulating blood and become filled with fluid (pulmonary edema). This can lead to unsafe decreases in the patient's blood pressure and oxygen levels. Sometimes, extra fluid can accumulate around the kidneys, known as hydronephrosis. As much as 22 liters of fluid have been removed from around the kidneys.

Our heart, liver, and kidneys are truly miracles and essential to survival. They automatically carry out millions of processes a day to keep us healthy, safe, and thriving. Although disease may alter function, we can often restore health through medications. If either one of these organs fails, we miraculously can transplant the organ of another person into the diseased individual, restoring nearly immediate balance to the body. This is truly a miracle!

Spiritual Dropsy

The irony of physical dropsy is that although the body has an excess of total body water, the excess of water is unusable to the rest of the body. Edema is fluid that is outside circulation. Not only does excess fluid not contribute meaningfully to our well-being, such as in the case of pleural effusion, pulmonary edema, or ascites, but it can also be damaging to our bodies.

Jesus and His Gospel are frequently compared to a fountain of living water. When living water flows, the people can come and partake of the water freely. However, they were forced to store water in cisterns without running water. The prophet Jeremiah warned of the spiritual peril that would result by forsaking available living water and instead relying on our stored-up but stale cisterns that became broken and cracked and could hold no water.[1] Just as our physical bodies require fresh daily water, so do our spirits. Daily experiences with the Holy Ghost are crucial to our spiritual survival. The people of Nephi recognized this. After the Savior had visited them and they were preparing for him to return, it states, "And they did pray for that which they most desired; and they desired that the Holy Ghost should be given unto them."[2] Of all the things they could pray for, including that the Savior would appear unto them again, they recognized the essential role that living in the Spirit plays in their spiritual survival. Consider just a few of the blessings of the Holy Ghost.

- guides us to the truth and bears witness of that truth[3]
- enlightens our minds and fills us with joy[4]
- quickens our understanding[5]
- speaks peace to our mind and heart[6]
- purifies and sanctifies our hearts[7]
- tell us all things we should do[8]
- shows all things we should do[9]
- brings all things to Remembrance[10]
- teaches all things[11]
- is the source of love, peace, joy, comfort, patience, meekness, gentleness, faith, and hope[12]

It should be no wonder then why the first prophet of this dispensation, Joseph Smith, came in vision to Brigham Young and emphatically stated, "Tell the brethren to be humble and faithful and be sure to keep the Spirit of the Lord, that it will lead them aright."[13]

Similarly, our modern prophet, President Nelson, has urged,

> "In coming days, it will not be possible to survive spiritually without the guiding, directing, comforting, and constant influence of the Holy Ghost. My beloved brothers and sisters, I plead with you to increase your spiritual capacity to receive revelation."[14]

We can no longer live on the borrowed light of our past. It is entirely inadequate to proceed through life expecting to only draw upon our spiritual cisterns of the past to quench the parched lips of the trials, afflictions, and challenges of the present and future. The fire felt while serving a mission will fade to nothing more than a flickering flame snuffed out by the winds of adversity without consistent, meaningful moments of feeling and recognizing the companionship of the Holy Ghost.

Often in our yearning to quench our spiritual thirst, we may neglect to partake of living water and mistakenly search for sustenance that doesn't satisfy. Instead of turning to God for answers to the questions of our soul, we may conversely fill our time and minds with the opinions of others. Elder Kevin W. Pearson counsels,

> "We would do well to spend more time in meaningful conversation discussing our concerns with a loving Father in Heaven and less time seeking the opinions of other voices. We could also choose to change our daily news feed to the words of Christ in the holy scriptures and to prophetic words of His living prophets."[15]

Nowadays, many outlets compete to become our information source of truth. These voices persuade us to focus our limited time and efforts away from sources of eternal significance. However, like dropsy, these sources may fill us with useless information that can adversely affect our spiritual circulation and damage our spiritual progression and development. Unlike living waters of truth flowing directly from the Savior through the scriptures, words of the modern-day apostles and prophets, or personal revelation through the gift of the Holy Ghost, these counterfeits distract us from the source of real truth. They fill our spiritual cisterns with insignificant knowledge. Elder David P. Homer teaches,

> "We live in a world with many voices seeking our attention. With all the breaking news, tweets, blogs, podcasts, and compelling advice from Alexa, Siri, and others, we can find it difficult to know which voices to trust. Sometimes we crowdsource guidance in our lives, thinking the majority will provide the best source of truth."[16]

Reflection
1. Consider how you spend time with news, social media, or music. Determine how to spend more time in the scriptures, studying the words of modern-day prophets and church leaders, and inviting personal revelation through the Holy Ghost.
2. Ponder the last time you remember feeling the Holy Ghost. What were you doing? How were you feeling? Determine to stop doing things that lessen your ability to feel the Holy Ghost and start doing things that invite the Holy Ghost.
3. Study the role of the Holy Ghost by reading scriptures in the topical guide or studying Preach My Gospel, chapter 4. Seek opportunities to invite, recognize, and follow the promptings of the Holy Ghost.

---

[1] Jeremiah 2:13

[2] 3 Nephi 19:9

[3] John 16:13

[4] D&C 6:15, 11:13

[5] D&C 88:11

[6] D&C 6:23, 8:2-3

[7] 3 Nephi 27:20

[8] 2 Nephi 32:3

[9] 2 Nephi 32:5

[10] John 14:26

[11] John 14:26

[12] Galatians 5:22-23, Romans 15:13

[13] Brigham Young, vision, Feb. 17, 1847, in Brigham Young Office Files, 1832–1878, Church History Library, Salt Lake City

[14] Russell M. Nelson. "Revelation for the Church, Revelation for Our Lives," General Conference, May 2018

[15] Kevin W. Pearson. "Are You Still Willing?" General Conference, October 2022

[16] David P. Homer. "Hearing His Voice," General Conference, April 2019

Chapter 14

Jesus Feeds the Multitude

On at least two occasions, the multitudes who brought their sick and afflicted to Jesus for healing became hungry. The first account in Matthew 14:15-21 consisted of men, women, and children, numbering about 5,000 in total. Although Jesus had departed by ship into the desert, the people flocked from the cities to join and him and be healed by him. Jesus was filled with compassion and healed all those who were sick. This personalized and individualized healing undoubtedly took some time. At its completion, it was nighttime, the people were hungry, and it was too late for them to go into the nearby villages to buy food. Jesus asked his disciples to bring their only food - five loaves of bread and two fish. Looking toward heaven, he blessed and broke the food, gave it to his disciples, and instructed them to feed the multitude. All of the multitude ate, were filled, and the fragments of leftover food filled twelve baskets.

> Matthew 14:15-21
>> 15 And when it was evening, his disciples came to him, saying, This is a desert place, and the time is now past; send the multitude away, that they may go into the villages, and buy themselves victuals.
>> 16 But Jesus said unto them, They need not depart; give ye them to eat.
>> 17 And they say unto him, We have here but five loaves, and two fishes.
>> 18 He said, Bring them hither to me.
>> 19 And he commanded the multitude to sit down on the grass, and took the five loaves, and the two fishes, and looking up to heaven, he blessed, and brake, and gave the loaves to his disciples, and the disciples to the multitude.

20 And they did all eat, and were filled: and they took up of the fragments that remained twelve baskets full.
21 And they that had eaten were about five thousand men, beside women and children.

In this second account, Jesus went up to the top of a nearby mountain to sit down after traveling back to the Sea of Galilee.[1] The scriptural account does not describe why he did so. Still, it was familiar to the writers of the gospels that occasionally, Jesus retreated to pray unto His Father, ponder, and be alone. For example, immediately following the first feeding of the 5,000, Jesus also retreated into the mountaintop to pray that evening. However, his alone time had been cut short because his disciples were toiling on a stormy sea. Perhaps this is why he returned to the mountaintop to be alone again.

However, this time, the multitudes followed him up the mountaintop. They had heard of the many miracles he had thus performed and so "having with them those that were lame, blind, dumb, maimed, and many others, and cast them down at Jesus' feet"[2] so that he could heal them. It appears that this also took considerable time because after they were given an opportunity to glorify God for the miracles that were performed, Jesus stated that the multitude had now been with him for three days. Given the account in the Book of Mormon that Jesus healed them one by one, it can be supposed that perhaps he did the same with those who came to him on the mountaintop.[3] His disciples reported they had seven loaves of bread and only "a few little fishes." As he had done previously, the Savior gave thanks, broke the food, and had his disciples distribute it to the multitude. The multitude all ate and were filled. Matthew reports seven baskets full of broken meat were left over on this occasion.

Matthew 15:32-38

32 Then Jesus called his disciples unto him, and said, I have compassion on the multitude, because they continue with me now three days, and have nothing to eat: and I will not send them away fasting, lest they faint in the way.

33 And his disciples say unto him, Whence should we have so much bread in the wilderness, as to fill so great a multitude?

34 And Jesus saith unto them, How many loaves have ye? And they said, Seven, and a few little fishes.

35 And he commanded the multitude to sit down on the ground.

36 And he took the seven loaves and the fishes, and gave thanks, and brake them, and gave to his disciples, and the disciples to the multitude.

37 And they did all eat, and were filled: and they took up of the broken meat that was left seven baskets full.

38 And they that did eat were four thousand men, beside women and children.

The Miracle of Digestion

Hunger. It is a universal emotion experienced by everyone. For many, however, it is more than a temporary feeling of discomfort relieved by food intake. Nearly 1/8 of Americans and about 1 billion people worldwide have insufficient access to sustainable food resources and consequently live in a persistent state of hunger or malnourishment. Although the earth can still give abundantly, getting supply to where there is demand still challenges the goal of eliminating hunger.

Two hormones, ghrelin and leptin, have been discovered that contribute to the start and cessation of hunger. When the gastrointestinal tract hasn't received food for some time, the stomach produces ghrelin. Ghrelin increases appetite, stomach motility to prepare for food intake, and salivation and gastric secretion in preparation for food digestion. This hormone peaks just before a meal and increases when the blood sugar level is low. When you have consumed sufficient calories and have adequately replenished fat storage, fat cells secrete a hormone called leptin. Leptin tells the brain you are no longer hungry. Mice that lack ghrelin or ghrelin receptors resist weight gain, and mice that don't produce leptin become morbidly obese and develop insulin resistance and glucose insensitivity.

The digestive system consists of the gastrointestinal tract - mouth, esophagus, stomach, small and large intestines, and anus - along with the digestive organs - the pancreas, gallbladder, and liver. Digestion begins even before food enters your mouth. As you see or think about food or smell the aroma of food, your salivary glands rev up for the moment that food enters your mouth. Salivary glands secrete fluid to moisten food, making it easier to pass down the digestive tract. The enzyme amylase is secreted to break up starches. Chewing breaks the food into smaller pieces, allowing more surface area to interact with digestion enzymes.

In a complex coordination between over 30 muscles and nerves, the chewed food is swallowed and travels from your mouth down your esophagus and into your stomach. Upper and lower esophageal sphincters relax to allow food to pass and tighten to enable food to mix without going backward. Once in the stomach, food continues to churn as the stomach contracts. G cells near the stomach's end called the pylorus secrete the hormone gastrin. Gastrin circulates in the blood and binds to parietal cells in the stomach that secrete acid to dissolve food further. Acid additionally converts the enzyme pepsinogen, secreted by stomach chief cells, into pepsin. The pepsin enzyme further breaks up the food into proteins and amino acids in a chyme substance. Meanwhile, stomach mucous cells secrete an alkaline substance that protects the stomach lining from the acidic environment.

As the chyme enters the first part of the small intestine, called the duodenum, the acidic chyme stimulates the production and release of the hormone secretin into the bloodstream. This hormone circulates to the pancreas and triggers it to release a bicarbonate-rich fluid to neutralize the acid in the small intestine. Furthermore, the pancreas secretes proteases (exocrine function of the pancreas) that become activated by the acidic mixture to break down proteins and fats further. As carbohydrates begin to be absorbed, increases in blood glucose levels trigger the pancreas to release insulin into the bloodstream (endocrine function of the pancreas), which helps transport glucose into the body's cells. Small intestinal cells secrete enzymes that break down complex sugars like maltase, sucrose, and galactose into glucose. The gallbladder, which stores bile, bile salts, cholesterol, and metabolized wastes such as bilirubin, is secreted into the portion of the small intestine called the duodenum. This allows for the emulsification of consumed fats that can be absorbed later in the small intestine, along with the essential fat-soluble vitamins A, D, E, and K.

The small intestine is a complex network of nerves and smooth muscles that spans a distance of nine to fifteen feet. As food enters a portion of the smooth intestine, it causes mechanical distension of the muscle wall and mucosal irritation. This activates nerves that release the excitatory hormones substance P and acetylcholine that stimulate contraction of the smooth muscle above the food bolus, promoting motility down the digestive tract. This food bolus distension also releases nitrous oxide and vasoactive intestinal peptide that relax the smooth muscle downstream of the food bolus to promote continued downward travel. This process takes some time to allow maximal absorption of nutrients. Nearly 50% of the stomach is empty after about 2-3 hours, with most contents leaving after about 6 hrs. After another 2-3 hours, 50% of the small intestine has emptied the contents into the large intestine.

Although 90% of the water has been absorbed by the time it reaches the large intestine, the remaining water and nutrients are absorbed, forming feces in the large intestine. Goblet cells in the colon secrete mucus to help as a lubricant as the wastes become more dehydrated. This protects the epithelium layer of the colon. Gastrocolonic reflexes prepare the body to empty the colon when food enters the stomach. Because the large intestine does not secrete hormones of digestion, it relies on the abundance of bacteria to break down remaining food into digestible material in addition to synthesizing vitamin K, an essential vitamin to synthesize clotting and anti-clotting factors, and many of the B vitamins that a critical to the processing and storage of energy in the liver. The colon is home to nearly one thousand different species of bacteria, numbering as much as 10^{10} per gram of intestine. After traveling almost five feet of the large intestine, the feces is stored in the rectum until one is ready to expel it from the body in a complex coordination of internal and external anal sphincter relaxation called defecation.

Jesus Christ: The Great Multiplier

Jesus Christ is the great multiplier. Not only did he multiply the bread and fish for the multitude on two occasions, but there was plenty left over each time he did. The scriptures are replete with examples of the multiplying power of the Savior. One of my favorite accounts is in 1 Nephi chapter 16 of the Book of Mormon. Lehi and his family were hungry because the bows of Laman and Lemuel had lost their springs. Furthermore, Nephi's bow, despite being made of fine steel, was broken. The families of Lehi and Ishmael had been relying on the hunt for food. When they returned unsuccessfully, they "did suffer much for the want of food" and "being much fatigued" began to murmur because of their afflictions. After doing the best they could with what they could control - Nephi made a new bow, collected a sling and stones, and turned to his father Lehi, the prophet, to inquire where to go - the voice of the Lord came unto Lehi. The voice directed him to the tool the Lord had given him to receive direction - the Liahona. "And it came to pass that the voice of the Lord said unto him: Look upon the ball, and behold the things which are written."[4]

To their astonishment, there was new writing upon the Liahona for the first time. They learned it functioned similarly to the pointers. The words also changed from time to time according to the faith and diligence that they gave to it. At this moment, Nephi realizes the multiplying effect of Jesus Christ when he states, "And thus we see that **by small means** the Lord can bring about **great things**."[5]

The equation is simple. Faith in the Lord Jesus Christ + diligence + Lord → great things. However, Nephi admits that "because of the simpleness of the way, or the easiness of it, there were many who perished." He describes the people of Moses who only had to look and be healed after being bitten by fiery flying serpents in the wilderness but refused to do so.[6] Alma said to his son Helaman that "by **small and simple means** are **great things** brought to pass" as he emphasized the importance of keeping and maintaining the holy records.[7] Furthermore, he continues that Lehi and his family, in addition to the miracle of the Liahona, "had this miracle, and also many other miracles wrought by the power of God, day by day."[8] He explains that these miracles "were worked by **small means**" but "did show unto them **marvelous** works."[9]

The multiplying effect came through faith in the words of Jesus Christ written on the Liahona. In John, we learn that "in the beginning was *the Word*, and *the Word* was with God, and *the Word* was God."[10] He further teaches that "*the Word* was made flesh, [and] dwelt among us, (and we beheld his glory, the glory as of the only begotten of the Father)."[11]

Jesus Christ is the word. And if by *His Word* "all things were made by him"[12] or in other words, "through faith we understand that the worlds were framed by *the word* of God,"[13] why is it so difficult to believe that through faith in Jesus

Christ and *his Word,* he can organize matter out of chaos, separate His light from our dark, and bring beauty out of ashes in our individual life?

As emphasized in previous chapters, the Bible Dictionary teaches that "faith is a principle of action and power" and that "strong faith is developed by obedience to the gospel of Jesus Christ; in other words, faith comes by righteousness."[14] Thus, we show faith by learning about Jesus Christ and his words, then acting on and obeying the doctrine we know. The result of these "small things" is that the Lord can bless us with great power. This is Jesus Christ's multiplying effect.

Another critical element in the miracle of Jesus feeding the multitude is that the disciples brought whatever they had to the Savior, withholding nothing. The disciples didn't return a portion of bread or a fish just in case they were hungry. They brought it all to the Savior as an offering. Building off the example of the widow of Zarephath that has been described in earlier chapters, recall that The Lord told Elijah, "behold, I have commanded a widow woman there to sustain thee."[15] When he came, he asked her to bring him water and a morsel of bread. She explained to him that she only had a bit of oil and grain and that she was about to make the last of it for her and her son to eat before they would die. He prophetically promised that if she would instead feed it to him, her barrel of meal and supply of oil would never go empty. Having faith in a prophet's word, she did, according to Elijah, and she and her house ate for many days. However, her faith did not end there. She continued to show diligence unto faith despite the eventual death of her son by turning to the prophet Elijah, who performed a miracle by bringing her son back to life. She then bore testimony of *the Word* by saying, "Now by this I know that thou are a man of God, and that *the Word* of the Lord in thy mouth is truth."[16]

The miracle of the loaves and fishes, Lehi and his family, and the widow of Zerephath are physical examples of the power of Jesus Christ to multiply our efforts so that we will not physically go hungry. Equally important is what the multiplying power of Jesus Christ can do for our spiritual, mental, and emotional yearnings. It is critical for those who hunger and thirst after righteousness. The Apostle Peter understood and emphasized this fact as he began each of his epistles to Saints, reminding them of the multiplying power of Jesus Christ. "Grace unto you, and peace, be multiplied. Blessed be the God and Father of our Lord Jesus Christ,"[17] and, "to them that have obtained like precious faith with us through righteousness of God and our Saviour Jesus Christ: Grace and peace be multiplied unto you through the knowledge of God, and of Jesus our Lord."[18]

Jesus Christ, as the great multiplier, can multiply peace and grace for us. Grace is an enabling power for the here and now. It is through grace that we "receive strength and assistance to do good works that otherwise [we] would not be able to do if left to our own means. This grace is an enabling power..."[19] For this reason, Elder Bednar suggests that any time we encounter the word grace, we can substitute it for the word "enabling power." This underscores that Christ's grace is not simply reserved for the end - like some desperate, last-second hail mary pass to win the victory over this life - after all we can do. On the contrary, we can receive his enabling power to accomplish what we need to do in all our efforts, from beginning to end and in every aspect of our daily lives. Elder Bednar teaches:

> "Most of us clearly understand that the Atonement is for sinners. I am not so sure, however, that we know and understand that the Atonement is also for saints— for good men and women who are obedient and worthy and conscientious and who are striving to become better and serve more faithfully. I frankly do not think many of us "get it" concerning this enabling and strengthening aspect of the Atonement, and I wonder if we mistakenly believe we must make the journey from good to better and become a saint all by ourselves

through sheer grit, willpower, and discipline, and with our obviously limited capacities."[20]

When we turn to the Savior, he will bless us with power. In the strength of the Lord, we will be blessed to accomplish much more than we could. This is the simple miracle of Jesus. Through him, we can receive and give grace. Through Him and his grace, we can change. Through Him, our burdens may be light. Because of Him, we will feel and experience joy.

Reflection
1. In what ways have you seen a multiplication of blessings in your life or others through small acts of faith?
2. Choose something small and simple that you can do to draw closer to the Savior. Record the blessings you experience as you strive to come unto him.
3. Ponder upon the things that thwart your ability to experience joy. Focus on the Savior and ask God to help you know how to experience more joy. Act on your impressions.

---

[1] Matthew 15:29

[2] Matthew 15:33

[3] 3 Nephi, chapter 17

[4] 1 Nephi 16:26

[5] 1 Nephi 16:29 (emphasis added)

[6] 1 Nephi 17:41

[7] Alma 37:36 (emphasis added)

[8] Alma 37:40

[9] Alma 37:41(emphasis added)

[10] John 1:1

[11] John 1:14

[12] John 1:3

[13] Hebrews 11:3

[14] Bible Dictionary, Topic "Faith"

[15] 1 Kings 17:9

[16] 1 Kings 17:24

[17] 1 Peter 1:2

[18] 2 Peter 1:1-2

[19] Bible Dictionary, Topic "Grace", page 654

[20] David Bednar. "In the Strength of the Lord," BYU Speech, October 23, 2001

Afterword

I hope you have enjoyed this journey exploring the miracles of Jesus and that you afford me grace with any errors of content you may have discovered along the journey. I hope you have felt His love and have been blessed with a greater capacity and desire to feel his influence and recognize his power more in your life going forward. Seeking the Savior and becoming like Him is the quest of a lifetime. Wisemen still seek Him.

I am a changed person after reading and writing about the miracles of Jesus. I want to make Him more the center and focus of my life. I see the beauty of the ordinary as extraordinary, knowing even the ordinary was created by Him for me. I no longer seek miracles to strengthen my faith in Jesus Christ. Instead, I recognize miracles as a result of my faith. The small tender mercies of the Lord are no longer simply coincidences. I have experienced the grace of Christ and have an increased desire for others to feel the same. I readily acknowledge I am not perfect. I continue to make mistakes and will continue to make mistakes. However, I feel a greater connection to Him. I have experienced his enabling power to continue trying. I have felt his power to forgive. To uplift. To heal. To strengthen. I feel his love for me and His love for others. I recognize the light of Christ is in everything and that because of Him, I can see things more clearly. Not just with physical eyes but spiritual eyes, too. Through Him, and because of Him, I feel joy.

About the Author

Jared K Pearson was born of and raised by goodly parents in Salt Lake City, Utah. After graduating from West High School, he attended Brigham Young University (BYU). After serving a mission for the Church of Jesus Christ of Latter-Day Saints in the Kobe and Nagoya Missions from 2000 to 2002, he met his wife Shersti Montague. They married in the Seattle Temple in 2003. He graduated from BYU with a bachelor of arts in Japanese, completed medical school at the University of Vermont from 2005-2009, and completed an anesthesiology residency at Stanford University Medical Center from 2010-2013, followed by a pediatric anesthesiology fellowship at the Children's Hospital Colorado from 2013-2014.

Jared and Shersti have 6 children and currently reside in Orem, UT where he is currently a practicing anesthesiologist in Utah County. He enjoys running, cycling, and spending time with family, friends, neighbors, and serving in church callings with fellow church members.

Previous literary works of this amateur writer and novice self-publisher include a poem, "I, Am a Person," published in the journal Anesthesiology, Volume 122, Issue 2, February 2015.

Printed in Dunstable, United Kingdom